33 STRATEGIES TO THE Money Game

DJ RT/HEMI & P. LŌS

authorHOUSE®

AuthorHouse™
1663 Liberty Drive
Bloomington, IN 47403
www.authorhouse.com
Phone: 833-262-8899

Published by AuthorHouse 06/03/2022

ISBN: 978-1-6655-6137-2 (sc)
ISBN: 978-1-6655-6136-5 (e)

Print information available on the last page.

Dedicated,

This book is dedicated to our (Suns)Sons,
Ja'Far and Tacauri
As God, The Father(s) we leave this wealth of wisdom
to our (Suns)Sons, with much love and honor

Contents

Introduction xi

Strategy #1 Getting down to business concerning You 1
Strategy #2 Picking Your Battles and Winning Your War 7
Strategy #3 Play the Pawn, but think like a King 11
Strategy #4 See the Details and Know the Entails 15
Strategy #5 Eagles don't fly with buzzards, and Wolves don't strut with sheep 19
Strategy #6 Picking The Right Mate, is a possible Checkmate........... 25
Strategy #7 You must look the part, and also play the part............... 31
Strategy #8 Victory and Success is not an Accident 33
Strategy #9 Use your Head to budget your Bread............................... 37
Strategy #10 You must Pay the Price to live the Life............................ 39
Strategy #11 Organize, Capitalize and Monetize 41
Strategy #12 Wear the Right Mask, to get in the Right Party 43
Strategy #13 Plant a seed of Money, and later have a Money Tree 47
Strategy #14 Be a dedicated and committed Hustler........................... 49
Strategy #15 Leave the slave Plantation, to reach your Destination 53
Strategy #16 A Baby step is better than an Adult with still Feet 57
Strategy #17 Trusting is good, but Control is always better 59
Strategy #18 Before you move, Think, Think again and Think some More 61
Strategy #19 Power is a Means to an End.. 65

Strategy #20 Acquisition and Mergers 67
Strategy #21 Pay your Debt to get out of Debt 71
Strategy #22 Your problem is your Solution 73
Strategy #23 Charge your Ls' to get an L, and use your L 75
Strategy #24 In order to Win, you Must play the Game 79
Strategy #25 You can't be a Sucker in this Game 81
Strategy #26 The Machiavellian Way 83
Strategy #27 Fear has no Place in this Game 87
Strategy #28 People are a Weight to you, or they are Wings and a Way for you 89
Strategy #29 Control and Management 93
Strategy #30 Financing your Lifestyle 97
Strategy #31 Money, Sex and Power 101
Strategy #32 Your Truth is the Freedom to Success 107
Strategy #33 The Upper Room of All Strategies 111

Conclusion 121

Introduction

First and foremost, I would like to thank you dear reader, for purchasing this book. By you purchasing this book only mean one thing and one thing only, you are truly ready to get your shit together! We most definitely understand that and plus we are with you all the way to the finish line, only because we have been there also. There was a time back when we didn't have our shit together neither. We were just two black men, or better yet two lost niggas trying to find their way and meaning in life, while we were fucking lost in this injustice wilderness call United States of America. We were searching and determined to make changes in our lives, and those changes wasn't easy. But those changes were necessary! Dig this! When you have kids and you are young*(still wet behind the ears)* like we did, or even at a mature age. The parent lifestyle will change everything pertaining to your money, your time and your thinking, because it's no longer about you. A lot of you niggas got that part of the money game and life all twisted and fucked up. Now, before we get into it, there are some serious things that has to be cleared up.

First off, we are NOT telling you to do what we say or did concerning your money. We are Not telling you to make certain investments, nor are we telling to do exactly like we did. And we are Not advising you to make moves like we did and still doing. We strongly advise you to seek professional advise from a legal and competent CPA, which is a (certified public accountant), and other financial institutions. We strongly advise you to get professional financial advise from well established financial institution to give you sound financial advise. We are not CPAs, we are some guys that were determined to make changes in our lives, and we did by making changes mentally. Nothing in your life will be different for you, nor for your kid's life unless you change the way you think now! But a lot of you make excuses, blame other people and straight up give your mind and your time to the fear of failing. And you wonder why you are failing! Because your fucking mind and your thoughts is set on failure. When you focus on failure you are programming your mind to strongly consider failure as an option. When you change your mentality and the way you think, only then will you change the way you see the world, and your place in it. When you change the way you see the world, then you will see your place and your space to perform your greatness. When you know without a shadow of a doubt, what you are and who you are, then you will stand in your place and perform in your Royal Space. You dig? This book is Not, a theory or made up shit to make you like it or force you to buy it! This book of 33 Strategies are from our life experiences, that came with the ups and downs concerning our life and creating a money cushion, having a better partner(*wife or girlfriend*), and being examples for our kids and our grand-kids. These 33 Strategies to the Money game, are like your 32 vertebrates of your spinal cord, and the 33rd is your Head. We will consume and fill your head, which is the Upper Room of your body with Wisdom, Knowledge and Understanding. So have an open mind, which means leave out all of that bias judgmental bullshit! Many of our people have been and have become haters, instead of congratulators. We sincerely hope this book do for you, what these 33 Strategies has done for us in this game call and known as life. Success Is Yours!!!!

#1 STRATEGY

Getting down to business concerning You

This is the hardest and most difficult task, and strategy for most people. We have encountered this necessary strategy, and we made money moves many of times, before we truly understood why we weren't moving forward. You see, your greatest enemy is You! But you have been taught, told and indoctrinated by the United States colonial powers that has used many of these strategies on black people past and present. They are still using some of these strategies to keep you listening to them to program you to be losers, with that slave mentality today. Just like the slaves back in the 1800s and early 1900s, you lost black man and black woman are still fucking slaves in your mind and heart, without you even knowing it, nor realizing it. The slaves are always forced to think concerning their masters, while they are being psychologically and emotionally forced to waste time on frivolous things. Now, you believe and think that every black man and black woman you see around you at the store, at a sports game, at the club, walking down street, driving a nice ride, living in a nice home, and making millions of dollars is your fucking enemy. No matter what another black man is doing, you were taught and told that is your Enemy! This why the white-man is winning in the game of business and having numerous of money bags. Another white man to another white man is major capital(money), businesses, big money investments, ownership and generational wealth. So, when another black man or nigga hate one another, what they have done and what they are doing is making it hard for them to be in business, and have a prosperous business. Why? Only because we hate each other and that forces us not to do business with each other. Can you dig it? If you believe that a successful person is your enemy, then you don't know what success really looks like, feels like and what it takes to be successful. When you change your mindset, you become strategic in all your affairs. It's easy to act and be a fool, but it takes focus and determination to be successful. It also forces you to learn about strategies and tactics when it comes to getting that money bag. If no one had to be strategic, tactful and seriously focus to get rich, then everyone would be rich. This is one of the main reasons out of many, why most people don't have money bags, saving accounts, a business and living the life they desire to live. They are looking for shortcuts and loopholes. That shit comes with being in the game for years, and knowing how the money game operates based on the rules, laws and the money system. When you look and focus on shortcuts to getting that money bag, you automatically cut yourself out of the money game. Only because you are training and telling yourself that you are not ready and willing to work, stay focus and do what needs to be done in order to win in the money game. That's a lazy and poor mindset! With that type of mindset, success and the money bag will always run from you, but you will get that chump-change. What is chump-change? The lazy person, the quitters, the cheaters, the losers, the abusers and those that make excuses type of money. In other words scraps! Usually these type of people don't have a savings account, money tucked away some where if they need it quickly. These types of people live pay check to pay check, and they also gripe, moan and bitch about there jobs, and without their jobs they would be living on the streets or living off or with someone that has some type of income. No one in the history of mankind became successful by doing and being the same person when they were at the bottom. They had to make some fucking changes and adjustments to the times, that political-economical fluctuating system, inflation and interest rates, the stock market, the organizations and the things that were happening around them. Here is why you have to get down to business concerning you. You stop you, you make fucking excuses for you, you blame other people for you, you argue with other people and yourself, you blame God, and some of you even blame your parents. They say *"the truth hurts"*, well got damn it get ready to fell the pain.

We kept banging our heads against the wall doing stupid shit! We kept tripping on a mow-hills of money and wasting our time away on stupid things. Hanging out with other cats that we thought were cool and down for the game. All of that fraudulent male Ego tripping was rubbing off on us. Now, we damn sure know why you have to be careful with the company you keep. Only because we kept company with those guys that didn't have a goal, no vision and they didn't have a plan for their future. At that time we didn't neither, that's why we hung out bullshitting, wasting time and thinking we were on some big shit! Blowing our money we had those setbacks, and sit downs in that steel cage that comes with the street life.

Those few experiences taught us when you don't know much, you can never do much, nor can you do and be different. The sucker that does the same thing day in and day out, will be the same sucker getting no where. Why? Because they are suckers. And you know what? Lame ass Suckers love lollipops, because the lollipops are sweet, cheap and easy to get. Real cats that want serious money, understand why they must do things in a certain way. That's why getting down to business with yourself is so important! You got to know who are, in order for you to know what you are built for. Everybody wants to be rich and wealthy, but everybody ain't built for it. You have to know what you are, in order for you to do what you were built for. When you don't know your place and your lane, then you will be in someone's way slowing them down. Not only that, you will be wasting your time, and getting older with nothing to show but one thing.

You are a loser! When you don't give a shit about yourself, you definitely don't give a shit about anyone else. By not giving a shit about anything and no one is how you stay broke, busted and disgusted. No one can win or use a good strategy for success with a shitty attitude! It takes a team, and you have to have a strategy in order to create a team, and make it move for the Team to Win. You can't be a strategist thinking small, making excuses, hating others for their success, and lying to yourself. You might have heard this concerning business, *"fake it until you make it."* Now, that quote has helped many people become successful. You probably saying, *"you just said don't lie to yourself, but if I'm faking it I'm lying to myself."* This is a strategy! How? When you know why you are doing what you are doing, then you will apply the method, which is how to get what you need and want from negotiating, being shrewdly clever and out thinking the other person or people. By telling the other person what they need to hear and believe it. This is how you get in a better position. Now, you don't do this to everyone, and especially not to your Team players. See life is warfare, and in warfare deception is a very imperative strategy to use for survival. But some of you, which is truly sad to say, love and enjoy lying! This is why getting down to business with yourself is important, and how you learn to see your strengthens and weaknesses. If you don't know your own weaknesses, then the other person will use your own weaknesses against you. That only mean they were strategic and you wasn't. Many of you have deluded yourself on believing you really know who you are. When you keep putting yourself in harms way over and over again, and you keep telling yourself, *"I got to be more careful,"* and you find yourself in the same situation. If you really knew yourself like you claim and believe you do, why would you keep putting your life on the line again and again? That's because you don't know who your are, and it's one of the reasons you are broke, and busting ass for someone other than yourself for a rich lifestyle. When you truly know who you are, and what you are, you don't have time for bullshit. You don't do stupid shit that will get you locked up for 40 to

50 years. When you get out, and see a world that has totally changed from when you left, now you are feeling some type of way and go back in. You have to use a strategy to find your way, and figure out what you are going to do. You don't put yourself in harms way when you see and know your value and your worth. When you don't care about yourself, and when you don't value your life, only then will you give it time for bullshit, dumb shit and stupid shit. We been there, and that shit doesn't add up your money, nor does it multiply your money, and it damn sure doesn't make your money bag bigger.

So, getting down to business is how to see what you are made of, and made for. You have to be a great thinker. You have to use your brain, and some people think the brain and the mind are the same. We don't mean to disappoint you, but the brain and the mind are not the same. That's another subject. Using your brain is how you get your life in order, then your natural born mind will awaken for you to become a strategist. This awakening will become your provider and your protector. But you have to know who you are and what you are. So, when you get down to business about knowing your life's purpose, all of your other business will come together like the yolk and the shell of an egg. Can you dig that? We had to perform this strategy, that's why we are successful in our field of business.

You might think and say that's not a strategy. We are here to tell you it is the greatest strategy, because you have to use your brain and think different and find the way for you. Dig this! In order for you to become great, you have to be better, in order for you to do different. When you don't know how, where, what and why to do something on a greater playing field, then you don't have a strategy. No one can get at the top doing stupid shit! Many have falling from the top, because they were doing dumb shit. Being stupid is not a tactic nor a strategy! When you don't change your mental method and your emotional madness, you will keep repeating the same dumb moves, and doing the same stupid things. Basically, you have to be a strategist by all means! A strategist is a person that utilizes their mental skills for a greater position in life. The strategist uses the art and sciences of psychology for planning ahead, thinking on a broad scale of life, using artifice, cunning, shrewd thinking for out maneuvering, outwitting and also taking, making and creating advantages. These strategies is how the strategist open doors for them to have more opportunities for their success and money. Once you become a successful person on the inside, then the money will come. If you stay the same person you are, then you will always be broke financially and still struggling to have money. And sooner or later money will say *"bye fool!"* Money demands a certain mindset and strategy in order to keep it, invest it and have more of it. That's why you have to get down to business with you, then money will get down to business for you. This is why we are businessmen today, because we did the most important thing to do, in order to be in business and have several businesses that work for us. This strategy paved the way for us to live the life we are living and have the things we have. We had to change our mentally and the way we thought about things concerning our lives. Then we had to take control of our thoughts, in order for us to take control of our lives.

#2 STRATEGY

Picking Your Battles and Winning Your War

When it comes to life we must know the difference between a battle and a war. Most people don't know the difference, and this is why we see a lot of young deaths, unnecessary fights, massive prison incarceration, and grand-mothers burying their young grand-children. What most of you *en factually* truly fail to see and understand, that violence is economical. And fools are paying the tab with their lives, their time, their minds and with the little money they do have, for the Power-brokers of the game. Check it out! When the United States went to war in Iraq, and prolong that war it brought the America economy to its knees. It forced Wall Street to create and make shitty deals in the housing spectrum, and people were thrown out of their homes from these shitty deals that served the Elites and Power-brokers' pockets. And Halliburton, and the other elite political players that were in cahoots got those major oil contracts, infrastructure contracts, and the political-capitalist capitalized big off other people's lives, deaths and destruction in Iraq and in America. President Bush's Administration understood the strategy of engaging the battle to win the war. When it came to picking the economical battle, they used Saddam Hussein's big-ego and hunger for power against him after using him. The battle was to bait, spy and calculate on Saddam Hussein's daily operations. When they truly understood Saddam's weakness, that's when they strategically moved in and won the war. This war put all those that were involved at the top of the fucking food chain. That powerful coterie of the 1% politically, economically and fraternally put themselves on top of the game economically and politically. What does that mean? Listen carefully to what happens when you Team up in the money game with real players for the money bag. It only means that the millionaires became multi-millionaires, the billionaires became trillionaires, only because they understand that violence is economical. If you committed a small crime and went to jail, if you could pay to get out, you would. If you couldn't pay you would have to stay, and the tax payers will pay for your jail stay. Niggas in the streets use violence for name and fame! Who's the baddest, that type of dumb shit! The white man is the baddest motherfucker, and that's why you lame dumb niggas don't fuck with him, or get at him like you do your own kind! Some cats use violence for drugs, to rob prostitutes, small range theft, stealing catalytic-converters and for small proceeds, that forces them to repeat the process at a large expense. Small fish in a big pond will always get eating and swallowed whole.

I also had to pick my battles to win my war. The battle that I had to pick was using someone's Dj equipment before I was able to get my own. Now, P. Lōs saw my skills and talent, and he pulled me to the side one night and put me up on game. He told me, *"Man you should have your own equipment and doing this shit for yourself. You see how many people was on the floor when that other cat was doing his thing, and you saw how many people got up and stayed on the floor when you was doing your thing. Man you know how to connect with people. As long as you know how to connect with people, and make sure they have a good time when it comes to parties, weddings and anniversaries you will always have you a side-hustle, extra money and one day a straight up Dj business."* He was right, and the battle I had to pick was to pay this guy a little money to use his equipment, until I was able to get my own. And the more I was using the guy's equipment the more he went up on the price for using his shit. So, this guy was winning the battle, but he lost the war when I got my own shit. Now, I'm contracted in various places and spots, because I was picking my battles in order to win the war to get the money bag. I set my own prices, and my customers don't have a problem because my skills speaks for themselves. What I'm saying is, you must know the battle you are engaged in and be mentally calculating. You must be a good listener to know what the other person or the payee desires are, and you also must know what they want, especially when it comes to getting the money bag. Most cats think you need a gun to win in this game. All you need is a psychology for business, a dedicated mind to one day be in business for yourself.

Play the Pawn, but think like a King

If you are a chess player, we are pretty sure you have heard the old saying, *"the queen is the most powerful piece on the chess board."* Well, we found that is not true. The most powerful piece on the chessboard is every piece that is moved from the power of the player's mind. Every move is a tactful strategy to conquer and win the game. The pawn moves in order to set the stage for the other pieces, in order to master and outwit those that wish to bring you down. So playing the pawn is to appear as though you don't have a hidden motive or agenda, but every king that was and is a king always has a hidden agenda for bigger things in life. If you think small, you will act and be small. Your body will follow those commands and those mental demands from your thoughts, your feelings and those strong desires to be what you seek to become. Whatever you see for yourself, you will be acting according to what you want for yourself.

There was a time when were acting, thinking and moving like pawns, but something wasn't setting right with us. So, when we sat down and chopped up, sliced it into many pieces, and looked at what was really happening around us, against us and for us. We knew we were born Princes and kings, and were acting like pawns without a strategy. We did some small things for a bigger vision. If you can't handle small money, then big money will never show up. Here's a little food for thought for you. When

I was in them fucking streets being a womanizer(player), and (D-boy), because I was feeding those heads their daily cheese. I was blowing money and taking care of one of my older brothers, due to his severe bad car accident. I had to step in and handle up with my money and time. Plus, I was spending money on worthless material shit and taking care of two households. I didn't have a plan for that money and that money told me *"Bye fool, you don't know what to do with me. I money, wasn't created for foolish things and stupid people. I was created for big plans, big minds and for generational wealth to come from* a *person who have big ideas and strategies to use me well over time."* That is what money told me, and I broke it all down for Dj R/T Hemi, and he grabbed that game of wisdom a ran with it without second guessing himself and thinking twice.

Of course, we gone to regular jobs like everyone else we know, but we didn't, and we don't think like workers nor like pawns. We act like pawns and workers, but we use our money like CEOs and our money is our employees. In other words, our money is our pawns, and our plans are strategic like a king to uphold the castle of our lifestyle. So work your job, just don't let your job work you! If you are thinking about the little things all the time, gossiping about people majority of the time, blaming other people for your issues you created and wishing for something bigger and better, then you will always be a pawn for the king you serve. You will never be or become a king, or a real Queen thinking and moving like pawns for someone other than yourself and your Kingdom.

If you are a follower, and you always worried about what other people will think about you, then you for a surety and a certainty you are a pawn. There's only one king in the castle and on the board, but there are many pawns in the castle and on the board, moving strategically for the king. He who is a king in mind, is a king with their actions and their leadership skills. If you don't know how to lead, then you will never have a Team. If you don't have a goal, a vision and a purpose for bigger and better things, then you will not make investments to become rich or wealthy. Every king that is truly a king has the gold, or better yet the money bag. If you don't know what it takes to be in the money game, then you will never have the right amount of money for the game. The money isn't for small minds, people that wish and hope, but do the same shit day in and day out can forget about having the real money bag. When you do the same you will get the same. If you don't like what you see in your life and around you, then you are the blame not us or anyone else. A pawn will always be a pawn unless it thinks it can be bigger and better. You will become a King by making the necessary strategic moves to be a King.

In order for you to have a strategic mindset, you have to think in a certain fashion for a big cause. The WHY, is always bigger than the How. Once you know Why, you want to be a King or have major money, then you will need a great strategy for wanting or desiring it. If your Why isn't big enough, then your actions will remain small. You can always start off small like all major companies have, and they call that start-up companies. See big companies started small, but they were innovated to be big one day from their Team players, strategical thoughts, tactful plans, certain ideas, thinking and envision themselves to being big one day. So every action, every thought, every invested dollar, every group meeting with the Team, and every strategic advertising campaign came from the Teams vision of becoming big. From the company's Team of great imagination, and their dedication to making their vision a reality, is like the pawn becoming a Queen or Rook. If you can not see yourself having it and living it, then you will never make a plan, nor a move to getting it. The Queen can make all kinds of moves for the King, but the King has to be very intelligent, and wise in order for him to have a powerful Queen that makes and does those acrobatic moves for the Kingdom. You dig?

Some of these big companies today started up in garages, in homes, in storage buildings, in the trunk of cars on city blocks, but their start wasn't their finish. They started with a vision and a certain mindset to live a different lifestyle. They were moving and acting like pawns starting out, but they saw themselves as money-kings in the end. Which means they were strategically thinking and making tactful moves, to come from nothing to being something. In order for that to happen you Must be a strategist in your mind, by your actions, from your dreams and with your investments.

See the Details and Know the Entails

Today you cats want control of your lives, and you want to have enough money to retire or live a certain lifestyle. But many of you cats really don't know how to take control of your destiny, in order for you to have the type of money you desire. To have serious money Young-blood consist of you making serious moves. Not by doing dumb shit and stupid shit! Dig this! You can't always think and act like a customer with every dime you make and with every dollar you have in your pocket or possession! Money demands for every person that wants much of it, to see the details on where their money is going, and you must know the entails on how to make more money. That means Young-blood, you have to be a strategist! Every serious nigga that was and is a hustler out on them streets used the hustler's mentality, the dope-game and the pimp game like a business, only because they are businesses. But according to the legal system they are illegal. So you must use your wits, to see the details that comes with the bullshit, and know the entails for you to come out on top. The way you use your money, will be the way you live your life. When it comes to being in control and having power over money, you must pay close attention to what you are doing with your money. If you are fucking off your money, then you will most definitely fuck off money someones gives you for whatever reason. Our focus and awareness was on the details of the money when it spoke to us. We all have heard the saying that, *"money talks."* Money really do talk, and if you don't know what the money is saying, that only means you are not having an intelligent conversation with your money. You if are not making strategic investment moves for more money, then you will keep getting and having the same amount of money. Money has its own rules, principles, value system and language. If you don't know the money rule, you lose. If you don't have the principles concerning money, you damn sure will lose again. If you don't value your money, then money will say *"fuck you"* and leave you, and that means you lost again. No matter what language in this world or on this planet a persons speaks, money speaks in that same language. And money always says, *"Use me wisely or foolishly. I will do what you the holder command or demand me to do."* The money bag will not come to you when you are not getting inside information, which is the details. And we are providing you with 33 Strategies of information with the details.

I was at a sports bar one night on the Northwest side of H-Town. When I walked in, it was only four niggas in the whole place. So I went to the bar. It was several women and men at the bar. Now, everybody that drinks know that wine is to be savored, meaning drank slowly. So while they were drinking beer and taking shots, they were getting fucked up quick. I was sitting on a stool next to this Caucasian gentlemen that was knocking them drinks down back to back. I was seeing the details and checking out the entails on how I was going to get men some bread before I split. While looking and appearing like the whole world was on my shoulders, which was all game! This Caucasian gentlemen asked me loudly, which means he was feeling damn good. *"What's your story partner?"* That's what the Caucasian gentlemen asked me, and I told him while appearing down and out, *"Well, it's too long to tell, and too short to understand."* He laughed so hard and replied, *"I've never heard anything that clever."* I gave a long story of bullshit, minutes later he was giving me $60, and I high tailed it out of there. Only because I was strategic with my words and my thinking. That's how I was able to get the money from being strategic. I moved around to three other sport bars that same night, and by the end of the night $300 was in my pocket. I played the money game like a strategist and received my payoff. Money comes to those that are intelligent. You cats better Peep Game on this Money Game!

Eagles don't fly with buzzards, and Wolves don't strut with sheep

When it comes to the global banks, major casinos, big money hedge funds investors, war-mongers and those clever Money Lending Businesses, they are the eagles and the wolves of the money game. The big investors are the rich and wealthy people that thinks and see business with the eye of an eagle. They also move sly and shrewdly like the wolves to remain at the top of the business world by all means. Because of their sharp keen vision and mind for success like an eagle, and their shrewdness is like a sly wolf that's why they have those large money bags. Only because they understand how to play the money game by using those ancient psychological powers from the 33th Strategy. The normal people are like the buzzards they wait for those filthy leftovers, which is like a job or begging. It's just enough for you to make it, but not enough for you to fly or rise above your money struggles. You will never fly with an eagle and move like a wolf in the money game, without the proper and necessary strategies. What they enjoy is power and wealth, and you enjoy bullshit and material stuff! The customer always act like a sheep! They are mentally and emotionally weak, and they give in to those material things and religious bullshit. That's why they are easy fucking prey to capture, and feed their weak fantasies and capitalized off their weaknesses and stupidity.

The banks know how to create money out of thin air. That's real game! The casinos know how to sell you shit on a free night slogan, and get it all back when you play their gambling games. The big hedge funds players have a certain set amount of money that has to be invested, in order for you to make an investment. Which means is strictly for the Big-boys, the eagles and the wolves. The war-monger, know how to create wars for profit, and sell you the image on television and raise prices in society. The big Money Lending Businesses, will loan you money, and have you locked in with those sly coercion tactics, and frighten you when you miss those payments. The contracts are so abstract in their meaning, but you are in a desperate situation mentally and financially. But you sign those clever contracts to pay the Money Lending Business back, when you don't have enough money for your daily needs. Plus, you don't know how to use your hard earn money! How can you repay or play the money game to win? These big money businesses utilize and function from these 33 strategies to you numskulls, and lock you in with your money over longs periods of time to repay more than what you borrowed. Since, you don't know about the 33 Strategies of the Money Game, they have been robbing and taking from you over long periods of time, with those high interest rates that forces you to pay 3 times of what you actually owe. So, in other words you are give them three times the money for one loan. What we just described and shown you is why and how these major players have the big money bags. They are strategist, with thick skin in the game and for the game. They are not distracted by material bullshit, but they know how to distract you and make a profit from and off your lack of mental discipline. The person that has your attention and knows how to get your attention, is the person that becomes your master and you the sheep, the buzzard and the money slave. While you work hard, they move smart, and their money works over time day and night. If you really want the kind of money these business eagles and wolves have, then you wouldn't be a hating ass lame, or dumb ass thief taking and stealing what's not yours. These 33 Strategies for money show you how to be slick to a can of oil, and receive those money spoils. Can you dig what we have put down so far? If so, grab the baton, and finish the race with these resources and across your finish line. With the right mind to be wise with every damn dime!

Whenever you go to purchase a car or home, and the finance department will try to find a bank to finance your purchase. When they find a bank for you, they tell you the bank is willing to finance you that car or home, if you put a certain amount of money down. Where is the bank's money to help you with this purchase? On paper it says the bank put this amount of money down for you, and you are left with the remaining balance after you have signed the contract. Next, you pull a certain amount of cash out of your pocket, wallet or purse, and when you signed the contract, you have to keep pulling out money from your account to pay the bank for a certain amount of years. The car company or housing department personnel on site gets the money with a commission from your down payment. So that means the bank has made a great amount of money from you without the bank putting up one dime. You didn't see the bank put down any money, and you see the financier who is the banker for the car company, and the housing business also works with the big global bankers. Money out of thin air! These global bankers utilizes this strategy to outwit you, and get rich off you. The bankers are the eagles, and they love it when a buzzard tries to fly with them but are unable. Due to the buzzard's nature, it is unable to do what an eagle can do. That is why many of you cats are unable to get off the ground, or make shit happening in your favor. Because you think and act contrary to your dynamic nature and mind. You act and think like a buzzard, and you wonder why your are not living and flying like an eagle. You have to learn from an eagle, in order to know what makes an eagle an eagle. It's the same with the wolf, the bankers wear polish and professional outfits, for you to trust them easily. Only because they look so clean an innocent in their white collar shirts! There's old saying in business and politics, *"there better you look, the easier it is to deceive."* See the banks know if you are a sheep, a wolf, an eagle or a buzzard. It all depends on the reason and type of business that brings you to the bank. If you are a borrower for personal reasons, you are a buzzard and a sheep, the wolf will eat you up alive with those high interest rates. If you are a buzzard, they will fly above you with a written contract and high interest rates, that will lock you in with them for years. This is the global money game when it comes to the banks. Can you dig it? You better!

Now, lets look at the casinos, and we will leave you wannabes with that. We know many of you lame-minded suckers don't like to expand your minds, or think outside the box. For one, you too fucking comfortable with having nothing and doing nothing big! You are afraid of change, and jumping in the big leagues of business and doing what it takes for those big money bags. But since you think small that's why your money is small also, with no investments to make it grow. And you don't have a money strategy to ensure that it will or have the potential to grow. If you ain't growing mentally sharp, then I know your money isn't growing and working from some business shop.

The casinos will send you an email about staying at one of their luxury hotels for free on certain nights. Some of them will let you eat for free, but depending on how much money you put in those gambling machines or how much you played on the tables. It is all calculated, which means all the money within the casino has to be counted for. When you play the slot machines or on the tables, all that shit they told you that was free, they got all back from you pulling the handle on those slot machines. The buzzard wish for a meal, and the sheep hope the wolf don't eat or slaughter them. But the wolf can only follow and be what it was created to be and do. All of us are in some form or fashion born to be great, many us refuse or don't recognize that greatness. The eagle and the wolf will capitalize off your vulnerability. So, you want the money bag? Learn how the Big Money players play the game. That's the only way you will be able to be one, is by mingling and talking with one is how you become one. Here's a quick strategy for you, that we have used when it came to us making those money investments. We would buy a money book from the used bookstore, and jot down some of the statements, and use those statements by asking questions to the business financial advisor or consultant for that business when we wanted to invest in. When you sound smart or appear to be intelligent you force the other person to be more intelligent or appear smarter than you. Only because they want your money to make those investments, by using your money to make them more money. Did you dig that? This is how you get more information concerning your money, and how you can protect or even grow your money faster. By utilizing those questions with clever words like we do and did. Here are those words of questioning; how, where, when and who does what with your money in order for your money to grow. This is another way to play the money game. Without a strategy you will get lost in the mix of the game, only because you don't know how to play the money game. Money is a numbers game, and numbers have to be strategically used. When you were in grade school they told you that numbers have a formula! All formulas are strategies and tactics on how to use numbers, to get the proper right and only answer concerning the numerical equation. Can you dig where we coming from?

We going to end this chapter, and put a little something on your mind. Dig this! Those wolves in the banking business, can rob millions of people of their money, less than five minutes without a gun. But a guy with a gun, can only rob one bank at a time, and possibly get caught. And he still wouldn't have gotten away with millions of dollars. Now you do the math and solve this money mathematical equation, you smart-ass!

Picking The Right Mate, is a possible Checkmate

When you first read this strategy, you had an idea but wasn't really sure what to make of it. This strategy consist of picking the right mate, whether wife, husband, girlfriend, boyfriend or the right business. This is a very, very touchy and important subject. Why is it so important? Because of your precious time, how the money will be made and used, the children's upbringing and their future, whether you or your mate will be successful, owning or investing in a business, and having a possible peace of mind to pass down the generational wisdom of wealth. Your mate can be your destruction, your mate can be your possible distraction, and your help-mate can be your loyal partner for successes in the money game. Especially, when it comes to check-mating the suckers that underestimate you and your mate's progress. Majority of you niggas or black people pick their mate from an emotional state of being. The big money players pick their possible mates by looking at their possible mate's family tree, the family's history and success story if there is one. They also take in consideration whether the possible mate's family ever owned a business of some sort, what's the possible mate's educational background, do you have any degrees or pursuing one, goals for the next five years, dreams for the next ten years, vision for a greater life, credit history and lifestyle to pass down to the next generation with wealth and wisdom. But niggas jump in relationships sometimes because they had a bad relationship before their present one. They do this to ease the pain from the old one, and get right into another one without considering the odds, the mental and emotional state of the potential new person or possible mate. Some niggas don't even think nor consider their actions and the outcome of their actions. The main one is unplanned kids, and using the person to come up. Some of us lack self-esteem, we feel we are not worthy enough to be with someone that appears to be out of our league or more successful than us. We both understand this without malice or hate. When you are young you do stupid things, and you pay the price to become smarter and wiser. Unfortunately, many of us don't wise up, we just continue to fuck up and blame someone else for it. Which is straight up lame ass shit, but that is what lames are and do! They blame=lame!!!

When it comes to relationships there is always an action and a reaction. The wise ones know how to be the source of action, and the other must understand with intelligence their reaction. Their action must be in accordance with the action of the wise one, if the action is for the both of them. This action and reaction must have an energy of respect, and a vision with a partnership in mind. If the relationship has the man or the woman singing their solo, *"me, me and I,"* then you have a selfish mate. This can lead to a fall-out from all the years of hard work and time that was put in. Then you are forced, and have to strongly consider finding another mate and start over again. One tactic is just remain single for a while. But no, some will continue to put up with that person's bullshit. Sometimes it's forever with some people to be single for the rest of their of life. Many of us, will start another relationship without some fucking inner changes for ourselves. Some will wind up picking another mate that looks different on the outside, but acts like the same person they just left on the inside. If you never been through a nasty divorce, you better ask somebody that has! Because if you are a nigga with no money, no people with power and influence in certain positions and in high places, in this white man's game of power and wealth, then you are a fucked nigga! Niggas be hollering the queen is the most powerful piece on the chessboard. Some of these lame ass niggas go as far and start calling these ranked bitches queens. That same bitch can be the reason you lose, only because you were not powerful with your actions, and mainly with your thinking and strategies. The queen can only be as powerful has her mate teaches her how to be. He must educate her on the money game, shapes her emotional understanding on the game, and plant those successful desires within her psyche to be powerful enough to make those successful moves. We are not saying that some women haven't been successful without a powerful man or without a strategic mate. That's not what we are saying at all! We are saying, if there is a man or woman that is more powerful in their imagination, thinking and has a vision for their success that's a qualified mate. If she is making those necessary moves for their success, then the male-mate should consider his position and responsibility to level up, or move the fuck on so she can be successful. Woman wasn't born with those powerful traits to make big and bold decisions over her male- mate, circumstances made her that way. Her power has always been to nourish the children, support the family and be a good help to her mate. When she is taught, instructed and told how, what and why by her male-mate to stand up and stand tall for them all, then she will become the Queen of power in her field and position. This how you checkmate motherfuckers in the game with a powerful mate. The game of money, power and sex has always been a chess game with a poker face, and the game of checkers is and always will be for them lames.

Some of these slick ass bitches will give you suckers all the pussy you want. These slick money hungry bitches will stroke your ego with their pussy. Their strategy is to blind you with their pussy, and hidden agenda buy selling game with their pussy. They are out to get pregnant by the biggest lame with money, and put his lame ass on child support for a check. Because the lame bitch is just as lazy as you are, but smarter than you were. Now, all she got to do is wait to pick up her check. She check-mated your bitch ass since you were thinking with your dick. That's what you checker players always want to do is jump on and in some hot pussy and brag about it, like it's some big shit. You suckers are always day dreaming at those Brazilian-butty lift bitches all the time. Just like playing chess we make strategic moves, and those moves take you lames out of the game, that you didn't know shit about anyway. Some of you suckers are in the way fucking up the game for us real players. That will never stop us because you suckers think ya'll know it all, but your actions say you don't know a damn thing. In business your money is your score card, that tells and reveals how successful and intelligent you really are. Stealing someone one's car parts is dumb shit, breaking in someone's home that's dumb shit and lying to a bitch just for some pussy that's stupid lame shit. Lames always do to others, what they don't want done to them! You wannabes are more focused on the ass, but screaming you want the money bag and the cash. The other half are claiming they want the money, but are spending their potential investment money on the shine and the bling. If you going to focus on the ass, make sure that ass is down for you, and you handle the cash like a businessmen or an investor. Because if that ass is putting in the work*(we not talking about pimping)*, and you blowing the money, that woman will stop your cash flow, and get down with some real niggas like us. You have to have a partner that has the same vision as you, and want the same things you want out of life. Then the two of you will be real partners, and handling things to be successful together. First, there must be respect for each other. Then, that respect becomes honor, which means the both of you must honor and respect what's established, and that leads to love. Next, you must love what you honor about the relationship or partnership and have sincere respect for each other and the money game. Finally, the partnership becomes tighter and the goal gets brighter. Now, loyalty is in the mix of this solid and unbreakable relationship or partnership, only if it is done correctly and established with some honesty.

When these powerful four attributes are broken and disregarded, then the possible partnership is broken, the goal is dead and the vision is lost in the wildness of hopelessness.

We mentioned having a male or female partner in your life to be your support, Team-mate or Team-player, your encouragement and also a stern visionary like yourself with action. With the right Team-mate and with some serious strategies, ya'll can make those great desires become a life long reality with those internal inspirations, imaginations and focused determination. We also have made some very tactful and strategical money moves for ourselves by partnering with, and also by investing with several oil and gas companies. We are not going to mention these companies at this time, duc to confidentiality. Basically, we make money day and night, because people are going to travel, drive around for recreation reasons, and some people have to work at night also. Lets take the eighteen-wheeler drivers, taxi drivers, Uber-drivers, or (tractor-trailer operators) with CDLs, that work at night also. So every time someone pulls up to a gas station, and put fuel in their car, trucks, vans, motorcycles and other gas operating vehicles we are making money night and day. Also during summer-time, when the lawn services are booming, and they are fueling up to use their lawn equipment. We still are making good money. Whenever people travel by plane or vehicle, and they need fuel. When it's time to change oil in those vehicles, whether you buy the oil and change it yourself, or even you go to some care shop to have it changed, we are still making money. Whenever the company expands their operations, grows financially, invent new ways to be innovative and prosperous, we also are being prosperous. Not only are we partners with these companies, we are also shares-holders with these companies, which makes us part owner of these companies. We get to vote on who we think, or who we believe is the best CEO to lead the company within these trying times of economic ups and down. Then we are faced also with those new energy-saving inventions in these changing times. So, we have picked our right mates and partners thus far, when it came to our personal partners, and also when it came to our professional partners with those innovative companies.

The strategy is to get yourself together, know who you are, be certain about your future, and be positive about what you want out of life. When you do this you will pick a possible partner without thinking with your dick, nor will she use her pussy. You will chose a partner from a new and sound mind, with a strong conviction to be sure of what type and kind of partner you want in life and for your well-being. Success is always a Inner grind first, before it rewards you with the the bling and the real shine! The bling is when your intellectual light comes on, and you truly dig the money game. By you making those necessary investments now you have financial longevity. You are not always going to be 20, 30 or 40 years old, especially if you keep doing that dumb shit. The shine is for that mind that digs and understands the game, and been anointed with the knowledge and wisdom on how to play the money game. The most important thing to consider is to invest while you are young! Investing money comes with tactics and strategies. And to get rich over time demands discipline. The more you invest your money into a prosperous small business, or a innovative large company, that means you have purchased stocks with that company. Now you own shares and part of the company for your money to start growing. Every time you automatically put money into an investment account for a portfolio that money is growing, so is your age.

#7 STRATEGY

You must look the part, and also play the part

Every professional business, major company and entertainment people wear their uniforms. The way you dress and what you wear tells the public, the company, the paying customers how professional you are, how successful you are, and also how well you are put together for business. Many of us love to look good without truly being professional. People want to look prosperous for show, but many of us fail to look good for business or even to impress someone we want or like. This is why this strategy is also important. Because many of you fail to look the part, but quick to act the part, and you wonder why you don't or didn't get the response nor the answer you wanted. Without the proper action on your part, that goes along with the dress code, you will majority of the time come up short.

Lets take a security-guard for example, when some people see a security-guard he or she always have their uniform on. For some people at certain times and certain places of business, just to see that a security-guard is around makes them feel comfortable. How would a person know if that person was a security-guard without their professional uniform on? Dig this now, by the security-guard being there in person, and by him or her wearing their company's uniform gives the public, the business their reasons to protect their merchandise and make the customers feel safe while shopping. Not only are they dressing the part, but they are also playing their part for a paycheck, and for the business to serve the public for profit.

When it comes to a salesperson, their dress code, and their words of persuasions is very important to the customer. To be a very good sales person, you must be strategic in your approach, your opening statements, in your demeanor, and most of all your dress code must make a statement of success and appear honest. This is what forces people to drop their guards and defenses. If you are unable to get people to be comfortable around you and be themselves, then you will never know enough about the person in order for them to reveal, what you need in order to make the sell. Because a potential customer that has their guards up are basically on their heels to dash in a flash away from you. You can't make a sell, if you are not strategic in your approach and also with your words. One of the greatest ways to sell anything, is to have a product or a service that sells itself. But you still have to play your part in presenting in it. Just like words and action go together, so does your manners and dress code go together. If you always told someone you were going to do something, and you never acted on those words. Now that person will take you as a lair and cheater, because you never fulfilled the action of those words. This world is built and created on a balance. Without the balance you will lose every time, because you fail to see the other side more clearly in order to apply the right methods and tactics, which are strategic moves and tactful mannerism.

#8 STRATEGY

Victory and Success is not an Accident

This strategy is strictly for the Big Boys, and not you weak ass lames! Big Boys don't whine, blame, hope and wish for their life to be bigger. They do what needs to be done, and what has to be done! The first thing they do is change the way they think, so they can change the way they do shit. That's why they always getting game, which is Wisdom, Knowledge and Understanding to put a strategical plan of action in place, and receive the benefit of using what God gave them to use, a clever Brain! Real victory and success come by the way of failures and setbacks. These failures are lessons with that Inner drive that always tugging and pulling on the Big Boys' psychology and inspiration. This Inner nagging is what forces the real players in the money game to keep their faith and confidence in tact. These so-call failures and setbacks, also shapes and molds the person to be what they need to be, in order to become what they desire and want to be. Strategies is a must when it comes to getting that money bag and playing the money game. See, many of you don't want to change, and you wonder why you keep getting the same. The Universe will never give a person something they can't handle or give them something too big they are not prepared to deal with intelligently. All that bread we had once before, we wasn't prepared intelligently, we didn't change our thoughts before we had the bread, nor did we make a change when we had it. So, that lost of all that money in this fluctuating money system was a blessing. Why was it a blessing? Because it forced us to make some serious psychological changes on how we handle our money. Those psychological changes we made truly helped us and it paid off. Those changes are still paying off for us to keep being strategical and tactful with our money and business within ourselves, for ourselves and our families. For us to keep making these smart money moves, we also have to be very tactful, psychologically clever and strategically intelligent for us to maneuver around those haters, that smile in our faces and also pat us on the back, while praying and hoping for our downfall. We know the reality of their hidden agenda, that they are plotting and planning against us. There has been numerous of people that inherited a large some of money, and there has been and always will be some people that will win that multi-million dollar lottery. Some of these people that received this large some of money, will eventual lose it all, spend it all by buying all times of material bullshit, and never learn how to keep it. One of the main reasons out of many, is because they weren't financially educated, nor did they have good sound money management, when they had the money to pay for those lessons on how to use money. Since, they didn't have a strategy on how to use that money, that's why they are broke and mad at the world. And the world don't owe them a got damn thing! What they should have done was give some of that money to certain smart money people to handle or invest it for them. They should have given some of that money to certain charities, and really try to help some people. The Universe would have given them some of that money back. Like the old money saying goes, "*money in a fool's hands' will soon depart.*" That's why there has never and never will be someone that will become successful or achieve a true victory by accident.

Accidents are something that wasn't planned, and it happened for a great cause. There is no such thing as an accident in this Universe. Everything happens for a great reason, a cause and a purpose. Not everyone will look into their situation to find their solution. If, we would all look into our so-call accidents that has happened the cause for it will reveal itself! The reason for it will show itself! And the purpose for it will make the whole situation clear. This so-call accident is to bring the person to some High Awareness for a greater cause. You dig? This Vast Universe is very strategic, tactful and abstract on what It shows and tells us. How can a person become very successful or achieve a real victory, when they didn't plan to be victorious, nor did they make any successful moves from the start? We will leave that question with you.

#9 STRATEGY

Use your Head to budget your Bread

This is one of the most single important factor concerning money when it comes to strategies and to the money game. This strategy is useless, if you don't change your mindset first and foremost. This strategy shows where your money is going after you have put all of your expenses on paper. This is a money trail for you to calculate the money that's coming in and going out. That way you are able to see how much money you are left with. Now, the money you are left with, plays a major factor on your future, and your future depends on your mindset. Like for instance, we pay ourselves first and foremost, before we pay any bill collector. Why? Dig this! Because we worked for it, we earned it, we are being smart about our money. When we pay ourselves first, we save that money in order to invest that money. If we don't see any good investments for us, we let the money remain in the saving-investing account, or sometimes we reward our partners for their due diligence and Team loyalty. You dig?

Every business has a budget, which means the business has to have a budget sheet in order to control, and see the unwarranted expenses for the business to make a profit and remain operational. All businesses are in business to serve and provide a product for profit to the public. Every house-hold or better yet, every employee or worker, especially if you are black should be doing this right Now! Not tomorrow, right Now!

If you don't use your head intelligently, then nothing will work for you productively. We all know that spending money is a major factor of life. When it comes to money and what you spend your money on plays a major factor in the money game. How much money you spend also is a major factor of life. If you are unable to keep much of your money, then you damn sure will not be able to do much in your life. You can only do what you want in life, according to the amount of money you have. If you don't have much, then you can't do much of anything. And whose fault is that? Damn sure isn't ours!

They way some of you use and spend your money, is so careless that it is appalling! What we mean is, many of you spend money emotionally, and that forces you to buy things that are worthless. That's why there is always a store that sells worthless and cheap things to small minded people. Lets get at our black women, not all them they know who they are. They will spend $2,000 on a purse, and can't $2,000 in their bank account. Then they are forced to have numerous of credit cards, that they are unable to pay off. This usually leads to maxing out the credit card, being in debt, being an economical slave and also having a fucked up credit score. Credit is the masterful way to play the money game! Whether it's a man or woman, the person that spends their money on bullshit are emotional spenders. This is what we call emotional-ignorance. Them young cats will spend their money on rims, cars, jewelry and liquor, just to impress a female or floss in front of another nigga that he hates. This is what we call emotional ego-tripping. When you don't use your head, you can never get ahead to be a head. Here is the emotional negative sequel starting from the person's emotional mindset. Negative thoughts can only produce negative feelings and results. Those negative thoughts and feelings will be the outcome of your actions, and those actions determines what you get back, or what your future will be. A head without big ideas, is a dead head without bread.

#10 STRATEGY

You must Pay the Price to live the Life

All the finer things in life comes with a price! The price is what are you willing to pay in order for you to have it? You must pay the price to achieve a greater life. You must pay the price to be more successful than you are now. You must pay the price to own that business, or to get the business on its feet up and running. You must pay the price! Now, paying the price doesn't actually mean a price tag. You dig? The price is, what are you willing to do to make things happen in your favor! Are you willing to work overtime on your job, and save up the money to invest it? Are you willing to give up the club life, and save that money to invest in yourself? Are you willing to buy books that will feed your mind and fire up your aspirations to be better? Are you willing to change your outlook and mindset to get it, have it and be an example for your kids and your community? You must pay the price! The luxury life, the rich lifestyle and the money bag, isn't going to fall out of the fucking sky, or show up at your door step, unless you pay the price for it to come to you that way. There are three types of people in this world, and one are very successful, rich and wealthy people. The other people are complacent and the last and third are straight up afraid. The people that make shit happen are strategically rich, wealthy or successful for making things happen in their favor. The second type of people are always watching what has happened. The third and last type of people are those that talk about what has happened. If you are the second or the third type, you got some serious work to do! The price is heavy and never cheap. Here's why the saying, "Game is sold, and not told" is so fucking True and Real!

#11 STRATEGY

Organize, Capitalize and Monetize

The main reason why there isn't many black businesses and black entrepreneurs today in the black neighborhoods and communities compared to our Ancestors that build "Black Wall Street", in Tulsa, Oklahoma and Durham, North Carolina, is because we are not organized. Not a single person, nor a group of people, nor a Team will never build or create a business from a person or people without being organized first and foremost. Our thinking is fucked up concerning one another. A brain that isn't trained or disciplined is a person without goals, no dreams, no vision. That is a person that's all over the place emotionally and psychologically. Dig this! Nothing around you will ever be organized or productive, if you are not organized within yourself first. Dig this! You are the mirror of the world around you, and the world you live in, is the space you occupy and have your being with expression. No one can never capitalize from an idea, if their thinking is not organized. You can't capitalize from an idea, if you are not focused, and you surely will not monetize an idea to profit from it, if you are not organized. When you get organized mentally, this is when your creative mental discipline and great aspirations comes to play a part to act on what you desire. To capitalize is to invest in yourself, which is that Inner idea to create or build something. You will began to think and feel that capitalist genius come alive with those needed strategies and tactics to monetize your visions and goals. You can't be afraid to invest in yourself! Fear is the lack of faith and belief in yourself! You are the one yelling and screaming what you want, and yet you are afraid to act. The money bag isn't for you. We organized, we capitalized and we monetized our ideas!

Wear the Right Mask, to get in the Right Party

We all wear a mask to disguised who we really are, in order to dupe or deceive the other person, in order to know who we are dealing with. When it comes to money you must play the game the same way, but you must be very tactful and certainly strategic. If you are not wearing the right mask to get in the right money party, where the people are having things and doing big things, then you will be left out. Here's what you must understand now and forever! The workers are the bottom feeders, and they are also the ones that holds up the platform for the rich. The rich holds the curtains for the wealthy, while the wealthy holds the lights for the powerful elite. This elite circle pull the strings for everyone to play their part on this world stage of money, politics and religion.

Our Ancestors left us a clue with a wealth of wisdom for us to be able to endure today, by outwitting these human animals in our present time in this concrete jungle. In Ancient Egypt, during an initiation ceremony these wise men would a wear certain types of animal mask for psychological purposes. Those initiations with the animal mask were spiritual and psychological ceremonies with a drama, to instill something deep within the psyche of the initiate. The head of the jackal would be the guide for the initiate. The jackal is part of the fox and wolf family.

The long ears represents the power to hear clearly, the nose is the power of smelling, the penetrating eyes are to see the object that is being watched and observed closely, and the small feet is for the agility to move quickly at a moments notice of danger in proximity. Aristotle mentioned in one of his books of Politics, *"men are political animals."* And many of us don't know what politics is, and what's the main operations for a political body. To be political is to use the science, which is the knowledge of knowing how to be self-governing for yourself and your people. You can't be self-governing, when you don't own or participate in your own economical system. The economical or money system is the main system that has to be in place to operate within the community and neighborhoods for our people and generations. Without this money system and the politics in place, black people and niggas will forever be systemically controlled by the same slave-master's children to be slaves just like our fore-parents were slaves once before. We know many of you would say and are saying, *"I'm not anybody's slave. They just got to kill me before I become a slave."* Well, we got news for you, they are killing you! They are killing you softly, slowly but surely. Only because they have given you the methods, the keys and the psychology to do it to yourself, to your kids and to other blacks for their economical powerful positioning. How? By using tactful and strategic *"social engineering"* on your ass! Which is nothing other than psychological brainwashing with clever tactics and strategic propaganda. Since, we don't have an economical system in place for our people we are still slaves, but the worst type of slaves. Because we have more freedom than our fore-parents did, and more ways than one to make some serious money, and utilize this economical system of opportunities today. But we don't know how to come together for us to have our own political economical system. So, the money bag will always be and remain with just a few of us.

You see wolves strut and flock together. They also hunt together, they move together and they eat together. Why? Because they understand that real power is unity, and unity is the power of numbers that moves in a unison, and in a concentrated body on a single object for a single cause. Dig this! We want you to really understand and dig this objectively. Now since these shrewd, clever, and sly wolves are always moving and hunting together, it's a way and means for them to be able to outwit their prey for the feast and survival. We are told, taught and indoctrinated to be independent, well the rich, the wealthy and those that are successful flock, move, operate, build, invest and create together. We are not saying that a single individual can't make it happen for themselves. If that individual gets to become rich, wealthy and powerful alone, you better believe they use these tactics and strategies that we are giving to you. We wouldn't be able to write this, if we didn't utilize some of these tactics at one time, and some of the other strategies at another time. All 33 of these strategies were used by us in order for us to see how we could open some doors for our opportunities, and move in accordance to our natural talents, life skills and Inner desires for bigger and better things. The word *individual* means to be divided or *(in + divid + u + al)* = in division you all, and the word division mean sections. Niggas call it a click, my homies, my partners, a crew, a gang and my niggas. Blacks call it; my family, my fraternity, my sorority, my business associates and our membership club.

If you are not wearing your mask, then you will forever be outwitted, duped and deceived by those that understands the power of the cloak and dagger. See, real power has to be concealed, because if you appear to be a control freak people will withdraw from you. They will not trust you, and they will hate or despise you. The person that wishes to be seen at all times, and heard by talking loud, is really a weak person, a vulnerable individual and seeking validation. Here's a pawn that is needing someone with power, with self validation, and most all a leader. This is when the intelligent person that sees an opportunity to capitalize on the weak. Even a shark will not devour a strong whale or another sea creature, but if the shark see a whale or another sea creature that shows any weakness, the shark will devour it intensely. This is the way of the world of humans and animals, learn them or be devoured with no remorse. If you wear the right mask to get into the right party, where the people have the money bag, you will receive an entrance and invitation. But you must play the money game, because the men and women that play these money games are serious minded people. They will eat you up alive, and throw you out on your ass, when they see you didn't get in by an invitation or vouched for by another person at the party or from the circle of people that paid their dues.

Plant a seed of Money, and later have a Money Tree

Majority of people no matter what their race is, their ethnicity or their geographical location in the world today, want money for one purpose and one purpose only. We all know we need money for our basic needs like for food, shelter, and clothes. But most people want money to buy frivolous things! In other words, they want to buy worthless things, that is known in the money world as stuff. Shit that will never put money back in their pockets, because it's stuff and it's not an asset. The reason it isn't an asset is because it can't access anything worthy or economical. What you do today has a great outcome, potential or ability to effect your tomorrow. So, if you are out there blowing money, don't be mad at us or anyone for your own stupidity and sick way of handling your resources for your old age in these economical trying times. No nation, no business, no religious belief system, no political body or machine, group of people, no organization, no educational curriculum or system, nor a civilization can operate without an economical system. The money system was created to have a certain control over society. The creators of this new money system have an extensive plan of operation for their people to rule over all other nationalities, all ethnic groups and confiscate land across the whole globe. Which makes them the fucking Land-lords over the world! Can you dig that? Can you really wrap your mind around that? They considered all the outsiders to be worthless creatures, and animals that need to be tamed and trained like cattle, dogs and sheep. We all have heard of the saying, *"it's a dog eat dog world,"* and niggas and blacks are eating each other while they are drooling from their mouths, and begging for more violence to commit on their own kind, while their enemy gets the economical benefits. Dig this now, they have build the jail cells, prison systems, juvenile systems and CPS system, and these systems were created to make money off our ignorance. Why? Because animals has and always will be a benefit for man. Whether for food, clothing, shelter, furniture and most of all economically!

Slavery we all know was and is a monetary system, and they planted that money seed 400 years ago, and their children's children have and are reaping the benefits. While the niggas and their children are reaping and inheriting poverty, hatred for one another, internal anger, dis-belief, fatherless homes, drug addicts and alcoholics while claiming they love their children. Then we have those sex fiends, that act before they think. This ignorance without the proper mindset leads to the lack of cautiousness, rather than the need of understanding and responsibility. This is how you create and breed hopelessness for a young future, and most of all no financial future. The trees that keep sprouting up and growing is the seed of hatred, the seed of destruction, the seed of madness, the seed of violence, the seed of mass incarceration, and the deep embedded one is the seed of thought that says, *"a nigga ain't shit!"*

So, if you are not planting a money seed, which is investing your money into something that generates and recycle your invested money back to you. Then you will never be able to pick money off the money tree. That's only because you didn't understand and you still don't understand, why they tell you money don't grow on trees. It's because you haven't planted your money seed, INVESTED! Money grows from your Tree of Life, which is your ideas that comes from you and for you! Can you dig it?

#14 STRATEGY

Be a dedicated and committed Hustler

Many of you really don't know what is a hustler, and most of you don't know what makes a hustler a fucking Hustler. There are three things that makes a hustler a real hustler in name and game. The first thing that makes a hustler a hustler, is their mindset to achieve what they set out to get. The second, is they never settle for less, when it comes to achieving and having a better lifestyle. Last, they know that when it comes to hustling, they must operate with strategies and tactics. That means using their skills, and never being sloppy or put in half-ass work. A true hustler know how to bounce back, when shit go side ways. The hustler knows how to re-up, if shit falls through the cracks. The hustler always know where, and who has the money bag. He or she knows how to play the game like a fucking chameleon, in order to get the money bag. You must dig where we are coming from with this! Being a hustler is having a serious and real mindset, and knowing how and when to play the game. If you crack while pretending to be a hustler your ass is grass, and you definitely are in deep shit! That's from the top to the bottom! We mean from the streets to the corporate suites. If you fuck up in the corporate world by faking it, and you get exposed and your ass will be black-balled from that exclusive world of real money, influence and power to move people and things to your liking. So, don't claim this shit if you never was or are in the streets!

There is a great difference between being in the streets, and being on the streets. Being in the streets means your life is on the line every minute, and every time you are in that concrete jungle with those vicious two-legged lions, gorillas and foxes. Being on the streets means you are only in the fucking way, obstructing the pipeline for the real hustlers to keep their shit flowing from block to block for those money spots. True hustlers know how to move around clowns and lames, we just hate when light-weights think they are heavy-weights, and they never really did anything strategic, tactful and bigger than their normal small shit. You dig? Do you really dig that? Being a real hustler isn't something you can turn on and off when you want to. This hustler mindset never leaves you, it forces you to become wiser, smarter and hustle legally for a bigger and better life, and also for a bigger money bag.

When a hustler is dedicated and committed to themselves, they never sleep. Even when they appear to be sleeping, their mind is in the game and on the game with strategies to move up the ladder. Real hustlers in the game, know that playing this game comes with a dynamic source of power. And this power is very addictive when you have seen and lived it, and also lived off the money proceeds. This game that is played by hustlers has an air of addictive power, when you have people moving for you and with you, to reach the goal and have the gold. If you are really down like two flat tires and with no spare tires, this game will reward you for being committed and dedicated. But if you are claiming the game, and you are dipping and dappling into it, then the game will kick you out. It will show you that It has nothing for you! And if you keep pressing and playing with the game with bullshit, then this game will give you a lesson you wasn't ready for, nor ready to receive those severe punishments for breaking the laws and the rules that comes with this game. Only because many really didn't know the game like they claim. This game is all about laws, rules and principles. Fuck the fame! The money game is not about fame. It's about carving out a spot and place for securing your future and your kid's future. Lets hustle some more!

We going to leave you with this, and we deeply hope you dig this, dear reader. You showed us your intelligence by purchasing this book. We all have heard one time or another, that *"Money Talks and Bullshit Walks."* Here is why real and true hustlers are always conversing with other real hustlers. Since, *"Money Talks"*, and real hustlers know the language of money! That's why they are always conversing with another real hustler, giving each other news they can use when it comes to listening to the money, and talking shop about money and for money. Now, true hustlers will always walk away from bullshit, dumb shit, stupid shit that doesn't make sense in order to make some dollars. Like stealing a car that you know isn't yours, and the fool tries to get away from the cops by leading a trail of cops on a high speed chase. This type of shit puts everybody on the road life in jeopardy, and babies that are in some of those cars, while a young fool or old fool tries to get away from the dumb shit he started. Real and True hustlers never put other people's lives in a jam or in a deadly risk for money. Real and true hustlers know that money is an intelligent mind and formula to play the numbers game. This requires you to be intelligent with some slickness. Never do real and true hustlers put strategies and tactics together by using dangerous methods and careless means that will cause them to be incarcerated for 50 fucking years to life for a fucking few dollars. Fuck Fame, we in the Money Game!

about carving out a spot and place for securing your future and your kids' future. [illegible]

We [illegible] with this [illegible] we [illegible] this [illegible] made. You showed [illegible] by [illegible] this book. We all have heard [illegible] another [illegible] *[illegible] Tells and Bullshit Walks*. [illegible]

[illegible] Twice [illegible] told [illegible] more [illegible] [illegible] of our money. [illegible] with [illegible] and [illegible] and [illegible] dollars [illegible] stealing [illegible] that you know [illegible] and [illegible] costly [illegible] [illegible] while [illegible] and [illegible] [illegible] and [illegible]

#15 STRATEGY

Leave the slave Plantation, to reach your Destination

This strategy is about making up your mind, and doing what you claim you want for yourself. You see a slave does everything for its master, and it doesn't know how to leave the master. Only because the slave has been brainwashed by its master, to always remain a slave. A slave doubts itself! A slave never believes that it can achieve anything worthy, and do some great things with their life. Your master can come and be in any form whether human, substance or thing. Your master can be your mate, your nagging wife, your selfish girlfriend, your lazy husband, your low paying or backbreaking job, your cheating boyfriend, your uncontrollable sex addiction, your money debt, X-Rated porno movies, your food addiction, your lying addiction, your excuses to never leave your self-bondage, your stealing addiction, your religious fanatic belief system, your gambling addiction, your self-afflictions, and even your fucking drug addiction. Some slaves beat themselves with self-pity, alcoholism, and the greatest slave is the one that doesn't know how to count money. Money is a game of numbers and a slave doesn't care to learn to excel. A slave doesn't know anything about finance and investing, nor is the slave concerned about financial statements. Learning about finance and investing is a means and a way to financial freedom to get off the plantation. A slave is uneducated, and the slave will make excuses, due to the slave's fear of their master to remain financial illiterate. A slave is down right timid, when it comes to leaving the plantation to reach their life's destination. When you are a slave mentally you will always be a slave physically and spiritually for another person, for a group of people, and slave to your weaknesses. The slave is a slave psychologically first, before it performs the duties of a slave for its master. And today, majority of black people are still fucked up with that slave psychology for their masters. When the slave master divided the slaves into different sects and classes on the plantation, the slave master was psychologically brainwashing the slaves by using one slave against the other slave. And the modern day slaves are still obeying their master psychology, by hating another black person. Today we call it house nigger against field nigger, which is how the slave master was able psychologically to brainwash the slaves to always think like a slave, in order to always act like a slave. And the slave mentally is totally depended on the master. The slave depends on the master for everything, without the master the slave would die. The master thinks for the slave! The master feeds the slave! The master houses the slave in the worse condition, if the slave is a field nigga, then that slave will sleep in a rundown barn. The master provides clothing for the slave! Versace, Louis Vuitton, Gucci and all the other material bullshit! The master teaches the slave how to be religious, and by obeying the master the slaves are pleasing God. The slave master teaches the male slave to be a playboy. In other words be a breeder without the consequences and responsibility of fatherhood. And today, niggas are just breeders, and sperm donors like their master taught and told them to do and be as a slave. Just like the slave master call the slave women black bitches! And today you slave minded niggas still refer to our women as bitches, like he called his women cave bitches. The slave is not concerned with living a successful life without making his or her slave master happy and rich. The slave truly believes that greatness is to see their master being and doing well, before they see another slave escape or doing well. The slave is all about making their master happy at all cost, even if the slave has to be sad, mad, brutalized and deprived. To kill another slave is a stupid act, and a economical loss for the master if the slave is productive. But if the other slave or nigga is rebellious, then that rebellious nigga or rebellious slave, is a dead nigga and a dead rebellious slave, which makes the master feel happy and safe. Then he tells his other slaves he set that nigger free, and he is gone on to be with the Lord Jesus, that died for him. And the slave yell and scream "A-man." Because of their ignorance and their religious slave indoctrination.

An intelligent slave always plots, plans and scheme for an escape, or better yet to run away from their cruel master's psychological physical treatment. The master always beats and whips the slave, so the slave can remain a slave, by remembering the cruel harsh beating! Even to this very day, some of you slave minded niggas are still slaves. It's deep down in ya'll souls and psychology, by the way you talk and discipline your kids. You discipline your kids the same way your master disciplined his slaves, which is your fore-parents. The master would say and tell the slave, *"I'm going to whip you"* That's the same shit you slave minded niggas still tell your kids to this very day! Some of you slave minded niggas even scream it when you get into a heated argument, and about to throw some blows. What you slave minded niggas say, *"I'm whip your ass, or beat the black off you"* The beating is to make the slave submissive with fear, which makes the slave believe and convince themselves, *"ain't nothing better for me."* So, the slave remains a slave until its death. When a smart slave comes up with a plan to help themselves and the other slaves. The slave-minded person will deny or try to convince the smart slave that's a dumb and deadly plan to leave the plantation for a dream that's not possible, for a blind hope, a wish, and a vision for betterment. The slave-minded person will help the master to keep you in bondage with them. Today niggas call it *"crabs in a bucket."* The smart slave not only plots and plans to leave, but it also pays close attention to the master daily operations, and see how the master is progressing from their hopeless life. The smart slave learns how to count and read, by getting close to the master, and acting like they are devoted to the master. But the slave's strategy is to use the master's weakness and trust, to put those clever strategies in effect on how to escape the plantation and never get caught.

Once the smart slave has learned and paid close attention on the dos and don'ts, then the slave plots their strategies on whether to run for it in the night or at a certain time of day. But deep down within their souls and heartbeat, they will achieve their freedom from poverty, from repeating the same old ignorance for the master, stop making excuses about the themselves, and go all out for their freedom, than to continue to live a life of daily misery and struggle. The slave prays and follow the North Star to their freedom. The smart slave also know there is a better life for them, and they will die trying to live and achieve that life of freedom, which is a thousand times better than being a slave. The slave's life and daily experiences on their plantation is a daily life of misery, backbreaking jobs for pennies and doing everything for the master. The slave know the master doesn't love them, but the master needs the slave to remain a slave for the benefit of the master to remain RICH. Once a slave begins to think deeply and hard about freedom, the slave is no longer a slave mentally. Because a free mind is a powerful mind! So who and what is your master? Your master is stopping you or hindering you from leaving that life as a slave. The person that never thinks and believe it can be free from their own enslavement and plantation, will always be a slave. Dig that?

A Baby step is better than an Adult with still Feet

Many of us wish to be rich, wealthy and successful. Before we go any further, lets look at the word successful, so we can get a better understanding. The "American Dream" has nothing to do with success. The "American Dream" of success is a fucking nightmare, because it wants to purchase your soul, and not your talents! Many of our people and others have also sold themselves on this staged psychological propaganda. This slogan is deadly, and many have sold out their people, their dignity, their loyal friends and their families trying to achieve this bullshit known as the "American Dream." America is not for sale, but the United States is a corporation for major investors, and for those with a capitalistic mindset. Success only means to set out, and do what you said you were going to do or become. Take for instance, we decided that we were going to be investors in our talents, that's why one of us is a prominent professional Dj and business owner, and the other is a prolific and professional author of many books, and a major investor. We both are investors in this United States of Capitalism, that is what success looks like and truly is. The money always comes after and never before! That's why we made mention of it several times before, that you must become successful first, and the money will reward you for making those successful changes within you and for you. No one can have a very successful relationship, nor can they have a very successful business without them making those necessary successful changes mentally. Having a very successful marriage takes work with a certain mindset and with emotional understanding. If you want to achieve having a very successful company, obtain a very successful lifestyle, and own a very successful organization will never happen, if you are not psychologically successful conscious about being successful. So, you must at least take a baby step to be closer to becoming successful, than to be an adult with still feet in the same place not achieving anything. But you are sitting around pointing your crusty finger whining, complaining, moaning, and most of all blaming others. If you are not willing and serious enough to take or even make a baby step to achieve something greater and better for yourself, then why would you blame someone other than yourself? You are the one that hasn't done a damn thing by yourself nor for yourself? A baby step is always better and closer, than a foot that hasn't made a single step.

#17 STRATEGY

Trusting is good, but Control is always better

When I was out there in them streets being a womanizer, better yet a fucking player. And I was fucking good at it! I let my women know that I trusted them, but I still had to be in control of myself first, before I could control the whole situation for us. The control was strictly for us to become successful, and make those needed good investments for us to live the life of success. This psychological control was a strategic plan for us to live a certain lifestyle of success and money. The control also came with strategies on the women and on the guys. If you are unable to keep people, and things in there place they will get and be out of place. Even when I jumped in the D-boy game, when my women chose to flee and say fuck me. I grabbed that cheese and moon cookies to get me some bread. Whenever I was kicking it with my partners, I let them niggas know, that I got love and trust for them, but I still had to have a certain psychological pull on them. Meaning I had to always be in control of the situation, and also have control over myself to not make a stupid move for a fucking dollar.

Whenever you are unable to control a situation or people, then you will trust them whole heartily. Not only that you will expect for them to know what they are doing, and trust them to do the right thing. But here's the fucking question, what is the right thing? Because you didn't trust your own instinct, nor your talent, nor your skills to be the leader, you gave away power, positioning and the money bag. That means you didn't have a plan! A leader without a plan, tactics and a strategy isn't a leader! People will always complain about their leader, when they always have had a chance, and an opportunity to be the leader at some point of time in their lives. But they will deny taking that responsibility that comes with the position as a leader. Dig this! When someone other than themselves take the position, they will be the unhappy villain. The new leader will always see how people at the bottom can be very ungrateful, and the people at the bottom will always see how the leader can be very strict, stern and most of all controlling. The leader has to be when it comes to the day to day operation for success, riches and the money bag. A good follower will always learn from their leader, only because their leadership quality and gene is already within them. That's why they are able to learn and recognize a leader that's in themselves also. As the saying goes, *"Game recognize Game!"* You must be a leader in some form and fashion in order to achieve what you believe.

Everyone is a leader in some form or fashion, but if you don't recognize that you are a leader in some aspect of your life, then you will never step up, and step out in front to claim and take what is yours!

When you lack the control that a leader must have, then you will never be in control of your destiny. That means someone other than you will be calling the shoots for themselves, and by utilizing your energy, your time, your skills and your talents for their benefit. You must trust yourself to be better, only then will that intelligent genius within you will come alive. If you deny that Inner genius, then that genius will forever be dormant within you, and that Inner Genius will not do a damn thing with you nor for you!

Before you move, Think, Think again and Think some More

Here are some important questions for you to ponder over with great sincerity! Do you know what you are good at? Do you even know why you want to be successful? Do you have a clue why you want to be rich? Do you know why you want that money bag? Do you really know how to be a strategist? The reason we put these questions before you is because, we have seen and still see a lot of you guys and gals moving strictly on emotions. Dig this! Emotions has their reasons, their purposes and their place, but emotion in this money game has no place or position to play when it's business time! Can you dig that? You have to be and think like a capitalist, and a capitalist is someone that uses their head, in other words, they use their mind tactfully and most of all strategically. Since, majority of our people were raised by their grand-parents and single parent mothers, many of us grew up making silly emotional-decisions from a Christian concept of what's right and wrong. Not only are you moving on emotions you are moving on religious dogma that was created, by the same people's family lineage that own major lands, businesses, political influence, and the institutions that print these English Biblical scriptures. Those powerful money bag families, don't give a shit about God and religion! Only because they created the religion and told us what God is and what God look like.

They know many of you are too lazy, and set on emotional belief when it comes to understanding the language that these Biblical scriptures that were translated out of our Semitic language. You ever wondered why the Roman Catholic Church is so powerful economically? Because they are a unified organization, and they read their scriptures in Latin, which is a philosophical political-economical language. Latin is the language of metaphysics, politics, economics, and philosophy. We didn't mean to miss you with that! That's why philosophers think deeply! We are not trying to convert anyone, nor do we mean to attack your belief system. What you believe determines your actions. If you were taught that *"the love of money is the root of all evil,"* then serious money will forever stay away from you. We all want to have someone or something that we love close to us! So money will never remain with you, because you don't love having money. You will throw away what you don't love. When you truly love something you will do almost anything within your frame of thinking to keep that thing or person you love. That's why we make money moves, because we love having money. The lack of money can never grant you longevity for you to live, and live the way you want or deserve to. Especially, if you came up poor and struggling everyday for your basic needs, and never having time or money for vacations, traveling and enjoying yourself with your family. What we are conveying to you is that emotion hinders you, and it will stop you from achieving something that your very Lord has put in you, for you and on your brain to perform. That's why your imaginations, an ideas and strong constructive thoughts that come from within you, is giving you ideas for you to do something big that enters your thoughts. But many of you were brought up believing too small in yourselves, and your up-bringing came from people that were unable to read, and were taught and told they must believe or go to Hell. *No disrespect to our elders.* They pass that bullshit down to us like rain falling from those dark clouds. So you and us are struggling financially, emotionally distraught, totally mentally confused and distracted, spiritually blinded and lost, but most all and assuredly economically broke and disgusted. With all that emotional garbage within your mental and subconscious mind, many of you are unable to get off the ground and began climbing your mountain for your greatness.

If you are not thinking before you make a move, then you are going to commit a great error or grave mistake. Because human emotions are triggered by what that person feels, and not what they see right in front of them. Lets take a woman that has had many failed relationships over, over and over again for many years. Usually her emotional brain state begins to convince her that all men are losers. With that emotional blockage she can go out on date with a winner, and she will not be able to recognize that winner sitting right in front of her. Only because of all her pass emotional failings. So from that point on, every move she makes when it comes to getting a man, having a man and keeping a man will be reactionary before reality can reveal itself.

When it comes to getting this money bag, you better leave your emotions where they need to be. Many of us, and definitely myself is guilty of letting my emotions get in the way of my business. We been there several times! We have talked ourselves right out of a damn good deal, because we were too emotional and greedy. We were pushing the line for more leverage, not wanting to make the same bad investment mistake like we did before. There was a time when I was dealing with a financial advisor about making this investment for my portfolio, and I walked away angry because he wasn't listening to me. This was years ago, today that emotional arrogance has cause me to miss $500,000 dollars! A fucking half of a million dollars, if I had made that investment! I moved without thinking, and the money game, is a psychological game of numbers, chess and poker. Just like in chess, you have to think three moves ahead before your hand even touch one of your pieces. You touch it, you have to move it! So, think before you make one move, but think again to see your second move, and think some more to see your third move. This is how and what a real strategist would do. A real strategist will continue to think days ahead, plan weeks in advance, be tactful a month long and strategical years ahead. He will, he has done and will continue to think, think again and think some more to achieve what he set out and step out to achieve and have.

Power is a Means to an End

Today, many of our youngsters, and so-call adults have power mixed up, fucked up and most of all screwed up. Power is not about being the loudest in the room, nor is power about being a fucking bully. All that shit is nothing but insecurity! There is nothing, listen carefully, and we mean absolutely nothing weak, insecure, boastful, prideful, and loud about Power. When it comes to power the mechanism or grand tool is nothing but confidence and not conceit. Power is intelligence and confidence that's works together to achieve the mission unscathed. The truly powerful person, is the person that understands why power is to be used a certain way, at certain times, and with certain people. If you don't know what power is, then how in the Hell can power be obtained by you and used for you? Power is confidence that is contagious to persuade people to your side, and have them lower their guards and believe in your mission. Power is understanding how to shape minds and mold hearts, so others can feel your energy and sincerity, that appears to include them in the circle of success. Power is wisdom, that means you are able to see peoples' motives, hidden agendas and speak their thoughts with clarity and articulate a vision. Power is knowledge and knowing when to act, or move in a position to get closer to the goal for the gold. Power is also intelligence, that means knowing how to obtain information, without being detected or caught in the act. When you walk in a room, the way people look at you or act, will tell you, if you really have power or not! Power has a great psychological effect on people's psychological state and also on their emotional state. So whenever you are in a room or entering a room, and people feel uncomfortable around you, you are projecting power. On the other hand, if people are trying to accommodate you in a certain form or fashion, and they are going out of their way to do it, then you are articulating power. The weak always will serve, submit and obey the powerful one.

Basically, power is a strategic tool that must be used very cleverly cruel! Powerful people are never in a rush, whether talking or walking. They rush others and put a certain amount weight and responsibility on their subordinates' back. Why? Only because powerful people are handling bigger things with a wider scope and vision. They leave the small things for those that are able to handle and deal with those small things accordingly.

If your vision concerning your life is small, then you don't have power! And if your vision and goal is big, and you are not acting on it, you still do not have power! You will be used by those that possess power by some means to achieve their end. When you have power it will force you to think, move and act in a certain way for a bigger and better lifestyle. The money bag has and always will wind up in the hands, of big businesses and also those large bank accounts of powerful people. See, powerful people know that money is a tool, that has to be used intelligently and also strategically. That's why powerful people always hire, build and construct their visions, goals and energy with other people that understands, what and how power will and can make their lives a thousand time bigger and better. Power is used as a means to an end. Power is the ultimate End-Game! Dig this. We are going to sum up everything about power, and it is a means to an end. When you are in a position of power, that means you have what people need and want. Power can corrupt you, because absolute power, is absolutely too powerful.

#20 STRATEGY

Acquisition and Mergers

Many of you have heard of acquisition and mergers before, we quite sure of that. This is part of the money game that the Big Boys play. If you are truly and seriously a business minded player in the money game, and you haven't made these types of moves several times, then you do not understand big business. This is one of the major moves that big businesses have made in the past, in the present an will do in the future as long as there are humans breathing, wanting and needing.

Niggas in the streets didn't and don't understand this, mainly because niggas don't see and comprehend, what they are doing should be handled like a business. Niggas and ignorant blacks don't merge, they short-stop each other from getting the money bag that comes with a large piece of the pie call acquisitions, which are assets. Years ago when I was serving that cheese and them moon cookies with those other cats or D-Boys on the block. I would re-up quicker and faster than them. One of those cats that was younger than me, but he respected my hustle, stepped to me. That gave me the upper hand and leverage, which is power to make more money and faster. He wanted to know how was I able to re-up and sell out so fast. This is what I told him *"Man fuck all that short stopping each other. We on the same block and other spots getting money. If we come to together we will make more money, save more* money, *and also have each others back."*

He was apprehensive at first, so I told him, *"Lets try it for one week or two, and let the game and numbers tell you and show you the truth."* I was being strategic by planning and thinking way ahead of the game. Only because I knew I wasn't going to remain in that game. I seen to many niggas get shipped up the river for years, because niggas was snitching, copping and selling to anyone and other cats were getting murder. That quick re-up twice in one week, was more money to save for himself and me, and the re-up money was always in place. When that cheese factory department, and the moon cookie supply was on froze, we still had enough money to chill. This is what I propose to him, and only because I didn't watch movies for entertainment like other dumb niggas, when the game was on froze. I was learning the game on money, mergers, investing, the influence of power, and having the right business associates from watching those Mafia movies and those big corporate hedge fund investing movies. Watching a movie for entertainment is a waste of time, waste of energy and it destroys the mental power of imagination for bigger things.

This is what we do today, and it pays us better and more money. When you have a team with other business operations, and you have some type of business operation for yourself, and you merge with another person or business your money will grow. By taking some of that money and invest it with the new partner, the business or the company that comes together the business will becoming bigger, better and profitable like the Big Boys in this money game. This is how a diversified portfolio puts that money to work in many different areas of businesses across the globe. That means your money and business is working. When some of your other businesses are down or moving slow with profits, you will have the other business that are moving progressively forward, and your return on your investments is returning to you some of your invested money and more.

Even when you get married this an acquisition and merger corporation. But they don't tell you that, because the dumb and ignorant will always be a great profit, a loyal customer and great spender for the wise intelligent business people. That's why when you get married theirs a contract involved, and he or she that breaks the contract has to pay with half or with everything they own. If you are a nigga without power, influence and money, this political-economical court system will give it all to the woman. Because when it comes to business, all salespersons know that women are the best and loyal customers. So, they know they will get much and a lot of money out of her from her emotional ignorance and bad spending habits. That's why they also say or read out of the economical Bible, *"will you marry her or him for richer or poorer,"* we just paraphrasing. Here's the thing, if your partner is poor mentally when it comes to being an economical partner, then you are marrying the wrong partner if you wish and desire to get that money bag. No one can live a good life without money! Unless you both have an understanding that money isn't shit to both of you, which means both of you are made for each other, because both of you aren't shit from the start and the marriage will not be shit neither. We know people change over time, due to this social political-economical system that forces a person or people to change sooner or later. Basically, a marriage is a form of acquisition and merger, and acquisition is the means of acquiring assets or having some assets, and merging, that means coming together with your assets with another person. Hopefully that other person have some assets also from the start.

If you are not merging, or performing a great business transition call acquisition, then you are not making money moves for that money bag. Point Blank! Whenever an acquisition and merger has taken place with two businesses. That means one of those companies needs backing, and usually it's the company that needs the bigger, profitable and durable company to survive. Dig this! The company that needs the stronger company is the one that was being strategic to approach the powerful company for them to make that business merger and become a more powerful profitable business. That way they can be bigger, be better and still make more money. This how you survive a financial drought. This is something most niggas don't know nothing about, but they are always running off at the mouth!

Pay your Debt to get out of Debt

If you do not pay your debt, you will remain in debt! The debt you must pay, in order to get yourself out of your money debt, is to pay the debt you owe yourself. What is that debt you owe yourself? The debt you owe yourself is to become financially literate. If you do not understand or know what money truly is, then you will misuse the power of money you have at your finger tips, in your wallet, in your purse and in your bank account. We will break it down like this. I asked a financial advisor once, *"When you see money, this paper what do you see?"* And his answer was, *"I see money! I mean what else is there to see?"* I told him, *"I mean no disrespect, but you could never be my financial advisor!"* Here is it, when I see money whether coins or paper, there's an image that always show a Head. We are not talking about who the president is on the coin or paper bill. The head on the coin or paper bill is telling you the person that's holding that coin or paper bill, that in order to make or have more of this stuff, you need an idea, a great imagination, and a mentality to visualize yourself with more money. Now, when that takes place, then the mind will work for you and with you. See mind is the creative energy, that works with the brain after the brain organ has organized itself. This is the creative aspect of the image and likeness of God. We are not treading the waters about religion, this is beyond religion. This is mind science! Because no one can create, build or make anything that there mind can't see the image of or the thing first. As the saying goes, *"Out of mind out of sight!"* No different from this book. We talked about putting a book together, we sat down and discussed what we saw mentally, and then the book came to fruition. We paid our debt by becoming money smart, and we visualized ourselves making money moves, and we acted on those visions we saw mentally first. Dig this! First the thought, then the internal vision and then the will of action. For example, if the mind of man never thought to create an image for an airplane, the airplane would never have been created. Since the mind of the man and the people that had a vision that was so deep and profound, it move them to begin creating, what they visualize to be real by their mental creation. This mental thought and feelings forced them to act with a strong will to make it happen, because it was so real in their minds. Now you have an airplane, transportation in the air. Can you dig it?

So, you must pay your debt, and once that debt is paid, then you will be debt free with mental and financial freedom. Basically, you will be able to really breath, and we mean that literately! The debt you owe yourself is why your are in deep debt with a company or person. Since, you haven't paid that debt, you will forever be in greater debt with your money struggles that nags you, frustrates you and angers you. These negative thoughts forces you to be negative and blame others for the debt you created and also for the debt you are neglecting to pay. In other words, your debt is your problem and your solution. You can never get away from you! You are with yourself 24/7, and because you are unable to eliminate your money debt, it makes it impossible for you to eliminate your mental debt. This is what the Lord's Prayer is all about, but they are not going to tell you that, because then you will stop believing the bullshit, and stop giving your money to a person that knows what you know not. Pay your debt, you owe it to Yourself first, and then your kid's future, and their kid's future. This is how generational wealth is passed down from generation to generation. It has to start with someone, and from somewhere for it to generate. You dig it?

Your problem is your Solution

The problem you have is the problem you created! The solution is also in that problem. You ask how? We know you have heard, *"the proof is in the pudding."* If you would just look into that pudding, you will see the answer and have your solution. But no, many of you would rather blame, and point your fucking finger before looking at yourself. The problem came from your actions that began with your thoughts and feelings that forced you to act, which created your fucking problem! We don't mean to be too blunt, but the true must be told and exposed! If you are unable to handle this truth, then this book isn't for you! If you can't handle a solution that doesn't fit your frame of thinking, then you will remain the same person with those same drawn-out actions from your fucked up thoughts! In order to change the way you think you need different information, and some insight from others that are able to help you and aide you with your solution. But because the truth never comes the way you want it to, nor the truth comes the way you want to see it. Why is that? It requires of you to do what you have never done, in order for you to see what you can do that you never have done. Dig that?

Most people run from their problems, some make excuses and some are afraid to make changes, and then they wonder why they are living it!

You created it, so you must change it! You can't change other people, until you change yourself. You are your first and your last project. You are your problem, just like you are your solution. Everything that grows is rooted into the thing that gave it life to grow. Can you dig it?

Charge your Ls' to get an L, and use your L

When it comes to life, we all should know that we will not win every time there's a challenge or situation. Those challenges that confront us are to shape us to be a winner. First, we must learn how to loose so we can learn how to win. NO! We don't like loosing neither, but we understood that we will not win every situation or challenge. In fact, we kept encouraging each other that we had to push forward no matter what! The truth of the matter, we were much closer to winning. So, we took those Ls' and charged them to the game of getting money. By charging those Ls', losses to the game we learned some strategies and tactics! These strategies gave us the leverage we needed for us to walk away with a money bag, that gave us some comfort like a bean-bag and courage with that winner's *Swag.* Can you dig that?

In this money game we learned and earned our stripes, took our scars, that came with those iron bars. By us going through the valley with our lives, we charged our losses to the game, in order for us to get those money game lessons, that came with those inspirational blessings that provided us with the game leverage. Majority of the time, we would use leverage in a negotiating deal for us to win in the money game for the money bag. Leverage is what you need to put yourself in a good position. Today majority of our people are missing the power of leverage, only because they don't know what it is, because they are not financially educated, nor are they pursuing their dreams. Small minded niggas and dumb niggas always want shit for free, instead of charging those losses to the game. Niggas scream it, but they don't mean it! Because they don't know what it actually is. For them to get the lesson, and later use their wits from those losses to spit game for leverage, you have to take those losses before you can become a Boss among Bosses. All the Big Boys and those serious minded players in this money game understands the dynamics of leverage, lessons and losses. Before you win a game, accept your losses like a winner. Then you must play a few games, with more losses and a few wins. And play more games to see why you keep loosing, and how not to keep loosing more than you win. So you put a game plan together, which are your tactics first, then comes the strategy! This is when you will have more wins than losses, then the money game will reward you with a fat check, and extra money to invest. Then more money will come for you to receive your championship ring with the bling. Because you did the damn thing! In business losses are not losses, they are your lessons! Those great lessons, becomes your great strategical angle of intelligence to use leverage to retrieve the money bag. In other words, those losses are forcing you to think, and think, and think some more. When you hate loosing, it forces your mind to think of a plan, and those plans become tactics and strategies. There has been times when we had to use leverage for a job that was paying us less than what we wanted. By us using the power of leverage, we were able to get what we wanted while working on a job. That was to get a higher hourly pay, so we can have more money to take care of our families, and save some money for us to invest. Just like the CEO of a company that use the workers, which are the capital(money) for the business. Since we were workers in a business we used our capital(paycheck) as our workers. All successful CEOs have workers and money working for them. We did the same damn thing with our money(paycheck) to have money working for us, which is our employees. This is what real CEOs, Pimps, Players, Macks and Hustlers do, we always flip the game after we learn the rules. You better take those Ls' like a Boss, if not, you will always be at a loss! If you are loosing, and you haven't came to the conclusion why you keep loosing, then you will forever loose. One reason is because your are Not learning, nor do you really want what you say you want. We know you can have it, we are living proof of what a serious mindset will bring you and get for you. If your mind isn't made up, then it's fucked up. A fucked up mind is a person with a fucked up attitude. A person with a fucked up attitude will always get those Ls', losses, and blame someone else. And while they are blaming, the other person is gaming for a win. Only because their attitude is geared to winning, learning and playing the game fair! Charge your losses to the game, so you can get your lessons to use as leverage, and your life will be a living testament and that much better.

In order to Win, you Must play the Game

Most of the time when you hear someone say, *"I ain't got time for no games,"* it usually comes from a woman. Why? That's a great indication that she has had numerous failed relationships with males, and she's wondering why she is unable to get a man, keep man, and not share a man. Well here is the main reason, brace yourself! Majority of so-call males today are just as emotional as women, and two emotional people can and will only create more emotional havoc. Since women tell themselves they don't have time for games, well baby we got news for you. Emotional males can only play silly emotional games, while serious men play the successful game that forces them to be serious, focused and play the <u>Only</u> game that will reward them. If that bitch or woman leaves that's her lost. Dig this! If any woman leaves a real mature man, he's still good financially and psychologically equipped to move forward like a shark. That's why successful men are always working on themselves to get their mind in a place to always be above that mundane bullshit! This mindset is what separates the men from those emotional males, from those blames, lames and males and females with no game.

If you want that money bag, then you have to play the game that comes with getting and having that money bag. If you didn't have to play the money game in order for you to have it, you would have it already.

Since you don't have it, then you must play the game. The first and most important thing in this game is your mindset! If your mind is not set on playing by the rules, learning those most needed lessons, taking those losses for those strategic moves on this chessboard game of success and money, then sit your ass down and get out of the fucking way. This Game isn't for you, nor is the money! Chump-change is for those chumps without game! The chump category, is the place and spot for you suckers that want the money bag and shit the easy way, by stealing, lying, cheating and robbing. Then when the same shit happens to you, meaning when someone steals from you, rob you, lie to you, you get angry and blame them for doing the same shit you did. That's a fucked up mindset! If that's the game you are playing, then you have to accept everything that comes with that game! You can't leave out what comes along with it. Every game comes with rules, and those rules are there for the players to remain in order, to have dignity for themselves and respect for themselves, and respect for the game they chose to play and participate in. Everyone that has lived, and those that will be born are birthed with a certain game to play, before they get to this place call planet earth. We will admit at times you will have to play or participate in several games before you know which game is for you, and which game you are good at. The bottom line is you must play the game, in order to win in life. If you choose not to play the game, then you will be played on, by those that are playing the game and know how to play on others for their win. We all are chess pieces(people) on this chessboard game call life on planet earth. That's why life has rules, because it's the ultimate Game of life. Since and because life is the ultimate game when it comes to living, you must play strategically with your ultimate best, with extraordinary mental tactics and strategies. There are some very shrewd and hard nose players in this game, and they love playing this game like we do. We love this shit, like a fish takes water, or like an eagle that glides in the sky! Can you dig it?

#25 STRATEGY

You can't be a Sucker in this Game

If you ever heard the saying, *"Game recognize Game,"* then you can dig why a real player will know right from the jump, if the person standing in front of him is a real player. It's the same with a serious business person, they can tell if you are serious about your craft. How are the players able to tell from the jump if you are serious? Well, they were once you, they were once where you are now. They didn't come out their mother's womb being a bona-fide player or businessman. That's why you can't be a sucker in this game, because that naive shit will get you eaten by these hard nose, serious minded players in this money game. When you truly are deep down in this money game, you know what to give them suckers which is lollipops and Tootsie-Rolls. Why? Because suckers love to suck to please their tongue and feelings, and the game always pushed them down, and roll them away with the sweetness this game doesn't claim. It will provide for you and give you a sweet luxurious lifestyle, but the game isn't played by suckers with those sweet feelings of playing the victim! This game is played and was made by those that know how to play the game with sweetness. As the saying goes, if you know, *"You can catch more bees with honey than you can with vinegar,"* Suckers play this money game with salt and vinegar, and they wonder why the game folds and shimmer up on their lame asses. Salt dehydrates you, and vinegar is acidic to you. Either way your ass is out of the game for being a sucker! You can lie and act like you are in the game, showing is proving. Suckers hate, perpetrate, inflate stories and keep up the bullshit, while the real players have no time, nor do they give their minds to sucker shit. Real players are sponges and not suckers, Know the differences! Check this out!

I had Dj function one night, and when I arrived with my helper. The club owner, my helper and myself walked in to the place(club). This place was okay, but the place wasn't my concern, the reason I was there was my only concern. That was to provide a service at a certain price. I know how other Djs did their business, and I don't and never will knock them. Anyway we agreed I pulled out my contract and the dude said, *"Man you got a contract are you serious? Man you go to be the only Dj that I know that has a contract."* Then he looked at my helper, that was smoking on a fat cigar, and the guy popped a joke about my helper looking like a "Mafia Don" with that big cigar in his mouth. So I said, *"Do you want me to still set up? If not, I got some where else to be in a couple of hours.* He already had paid for his deposit, so it really wasn't a loss for me. But because I already got paid for doing nothing, and the other money was going to come when I provided the service. That's why we know this game isn't played by suckers. So the guy signed the contract, and at the end of the night. You know what he said? He said, *"Man, you are a serious and smart businessman, and you know how to keep the people happy, dancing and partying. They wanted me to stay open another hour. I'm call you again you better believe that."* And the rest is history.

#26 STRATEGY

The Machiavellian Way

I'm get right at you lame ass niggas that don't know history, when it comes to Niccolo Machiavelli. A lot of you niggas are passing that story around and down that Machiavelli faked his death. That's bullshit! Machiavelli didn't fake his death, he was exiled. Diderot was the one that faked his death! That's the main reason you suckers can't raise up out of the bullshit, because you keep your mind on bullshit and wasting your time speaking on shit you don't know nothing about. Sit the fuck down, and shut up and go to class! That's because you motherfuckers are too lazy to figure out what needs to be known, and better yet learn to speak on shit you really know about. Lazy people want shit for nothing and free, the blaming people want shit the easy way, and them damn haters want everybody and anybody to be just like them, which is to hate everybody. The Machiavellian Way is to always be above that bullshit, and at the same time know how to use your position, your time and your mind to learn how to be a Ruler, a Prince or a King in your Kingdom.

All that senseless killing in the street show you that niggas don't know who to use cruelty tactfully and strategically. Cruelty used well keeps your ass out of jail! Cruelty used well makes your woman respects you, and in the money game cruelty used well and prudently open doors for you. We are <u>Not</u> talking about being a bully, that's weak sucker shit! The bully was abused by their parents when they were kids or they were bullied everyday by someone they grew up with. See the game of money and business doesn't respect bullies, the game gets rid of their asses, by throwing them in the bully pen with other bullies, so they can be bulls among themselves where no one cares or gives a damn, which we call them felons or inmates.

The Machiavellian Way is knowing how to be respected and not despised. When people respect you, that means they like you, and they will do things for you and with you. If they despise you that means you are doing something very ugly, treacherous and inhumane to that person. Now they wish death upon you, and that's not the Machiavellian Way.

Some people even said that Machiavelli was evil, they said that so you wouldn't learn the Machiavellian Way. The Machiavellian Way comes with clever tactics and wise strategies on the game. Niccolo Machiavelli pulled the veil off those political players, and reveal their evil ways. They have made the game rules for themselves to always remain in power, and also for those that are in cahoots with them to remain in higher places. These political players and influential business men do favors for each other, and also break those rules and label it "white collar crime." Which means to pay a hefty fine, and move on to doing the same shit more strategic and isolated to never be exposed again. The people that tell you that Machiavelli is evil, are the same people that are using Machiavelli's lessons. The Big Boys have used the Machiavellian Way, and they are still using the methods and means of the Machiavellian Way, to be a Machiavellian when it comes to getting the money bag in this money game.

The Machiavellian Way is never to spill your beans before you prepared and planned the meal. In other words, you don't tell the whole story truthfully, you tell the story according to how that person can understand it, in order for them to carry out the mission for you. We are not teaching you to be evil or dishonest, we are teaching you to understand that everyone is not you, nor do they see the world the way you do. Everyone is living their lives the way they see to live it. We all act according to what and how we see the world and our place in it. Dig that! Like we said before, if this shit is too heavy for you to grasp, then the big money game isn't for you.

The Machiavellian Way tells us that being deceitful, killing, lying, cheating, using religion for profit, and backstabbing isn't honorable for a Prince or anyone that desires to be a Prince. But you must appear to be decent, honest, truthful, religious and dignified. You have to use the appearance of these good titles and attributes. Dig this, if you try to use these honorable, good intentions, truthful tactics with all people all the time, you will fall from the mountain of your success, and you will be pulled down by other people before you reach your successful mountain top. Why? See everybody isn't going to play fair with you, so you have to recognize that and see it coming before it arrives to do you harm. That's why the Machiavellian Way is knowing how to be a fox that's clever enough to see and spot those camouflaged Traps. You must also know how to use the lion for those conniving Tramps and continue to be a prudent player. This is the Machiavellian Way to become a Prince with those business Champs with the money bag, for playing the money game the Machiavellian way.

The Machiavellian Way, is also knowing how to use flattery in the game of business, but your flattery can't be noticeable. If you do, then you will be looking like a sucker, and you will be taking or believed to be a dishonest person, and nobody wants to do business with a dishonest person. Today they are called and known as scammers! The person that is labeled dishonest in business, will be the same person lacking business, and will spend most of their time and energy trying to rebuild their reputation in the business world. That means you will be losing money, instead of making money moves for the money bag. That's why the Machiavellian Way is the prudent way, and a clever way to climb to the top. The Machiavellian Way informs us that there is NO short-cuts to becoming and being a Prince in this money game. Like we said before, for those that look for short-cuts, are cutting themselves short of the long money, and the big money bag.

Why? They are cutting themselves out of those most needed lessons, that will sharpen them to become who and what they need to be to remain successful or nigga rich.

The Machiavellian Way prepares you mentally on the game and for the game. This game comes with cutthroats, backstabbers, liars, cheaters, thieves, deceivers and all kinds of dishonest shit. Read this strategy again, we wanted to add more to this strategy. But we didn't want to over-load your mental circuit! We mean that out of sheer respect.

Fear has no Place in this Game

Fear is one of the major setbacks in this game. The reason why fear is so powerful, is because people do not understand what fear really is. Fear was created by the Creator to be used, and not to be hindered by it. Fear is a powerful attribute when you know how to use it. When you don't know how to use fear, you will be stopped, hindered and unsuccessful from fear. What is fear? That frightening feeling and anxiety of a thing, a new place, a new challenge or a different person that is unknown to you. Here's when fear of the Unknown will come into play, so you can feel that possible transformation acting upon you. It will come only when you haven't known what needs to be known until the appropriate time, which is when you made up your mind to be different and do different. When you do the same thing over and over, what is it to fear? Nothing! Why? Because you know what the thing or the person will do, haven't done and hasn't done, so you are comfortable with that. But when it comes to something new, that's when fear shows up and steps in to take over by your natural instinctive permission.

Many of you want to be successful and rich, but you are afraid to invest money, make the necessary changes, mingle among new people, afraid to talk among new people, and most of all afraid to be in a different place in your mind. Complacency and being comfortable is destroying your dreams, and your possibility of becoming successful and rich. You have given fear a home and place to reside within you and around you. So success and riches has no place nor a reward for you, due to your own mental and emotional design. We didn't let fear stop us! Fear helped us to become players in this money game. We knew if we didn't overcome our fears, the money and financial cushion wouldn't be ours. Real players play the Game, why suckers sit around talking about the game, and never do a damn thing. You can sit around and twiddle your thumbs, we got up off our asses did a few things and some. This book would have never became a reality, if we sat around talking loud, and not being about it. This book is proof in our pudding, that we are doing something, and we are helping you to become a better and greater you. We value success, respect the players, we respect the game, and we respect those that has given us the game and the opportunity to do our thing. If you haven't heard we are going to give to you, *"Respect will take you far up the road to success, but fear and ignorance will get you nowhere ."*

Another way fear comes at you is by casting doubts from your lack of you knowing and believing in yourself. Fear is the aide and also the help, as the identifier of your talents and skills that you were born with. Many people we know have had many good ideas, but they doubted themselves. You guessed it right, then fear shows up right in the midst of their plan and potential. By fear dominating people dreams and visions, their possibility for them to becoming successful or rich, it's a pipe dream with no substance. A serious and passionate minded person will never let fear hold them down, push them off the cliff of their dreams, ideas, plans, tactics and most of all their strategies to making money moves. Dig this, fear is nothing other than the excitement of entering into a new life and a new world. That new world that you must enter is bigger, and better than the one you are living in and always have known. You must overcome your fears and jump over your hurdle call fear.

People are a Weight to you, or they are Wings and a Way for you

This strategy and chapter is about confronting, recognizing, and removing the person or people that are dead weight to you. Your partner whether a male, female, family member, a mate, friends or even your job can be your dead weight that's holding you down. When you are not in your capitalistic or entrepreneur state of mind, then you will attract or socialize with dead weight people. If you are not trying to accomplish anything, nine out of ten times your so-call partner or mate isn't trying to accomplish nothing grand also. Dig this, *"two wings to a bird fly together and flock as one."* Anyone that has never attempted anything greater than what they have been doing and being, will not understand you when you are attempting and doing something grand. It goes against their mental-laziness, and also against their emotional state of comfort and complacency. Your dead weight must be removed or cut loose in order for you to fly. Too many of you cats let your woman keep you down, hold you pussy bound and pressure you to stay small, so she call the shots and run it all. And the reason you cats do that, is because you have no confidence in yourself. The other half does it to keep house pussy, and the other 50% put up with this type of bullshit, because he hates to see that female with another dude. If that person is trying to accomplish something and you not, they are going to flee, run, and leave anyway. If their passion is strong about reaching their destiny, and breaking their norm, they will cut their dead weight loose, and get far away from you as possible. Any person that settles with their present plot will sink to the bottom, which is an indication they are dead weight. Dig this, this is a serious situation that warrants a precaution that we will make mention of. If you flew on a Boeing 747 or any type of airplane, before you and everyone else boards the airplane, all luggage must be checked in and the weight must be checked also. Why? Because of the danger if the airplane is over weighted. See, even an airplane has to have a certain amount of weight in order for the plane to fly smoothly, and get off the landing run-way and take-off smoothly. It's the fucking same with the person that is suppose to be with you and for you, but instead they are holding you down with too much fucking unnecessary dead weight. It's dangerous to any serious minded person's mental and emotional state of drive for success and the money bag. Whenever someone feels strong about doing something different with their life, you either have to be a way, a means to the end, and wings for them to take-off, if you want to remain in that person's life.

Whenever you or your mate is seeking to try something that can be beneficial for the both of you, you better sit down with them and come to some type of understanding with some fucking encouragement. And it better be real and sincere! If you really love that person which is your mate, then you better be a support system, if not your relationship with them will be cut-short. Usually the person that leaves is normally in the right, not all the time. Some of you motherfuckers can be very fucking selfish for no reason! But the negative person will blame, and sometimes they will rudely interrupt your life with bullshit. They will be spiteful towards you! Some of them trifling bitches will put you on child-support just to be ugly, nasty and hateful! Only because you did the right thing for you, and you was trying to do the better thing for the both of you. And some of you trifling ass niggas can be just as dramatic and emotionally fucked up than some of these women. But the person that fails to change with you and for them, is an indication they are dead weight to themselves. If you are dead weight with the person that truly loves you, and they are trying to make a better way, and you hate to see them change for the better, you are not a way, nor a door and you surely are not wings for them. You are a hater and a loser! The money game don't open up doors for haters and losers. Most people fail to understand and even nature shows us the seasons, and the seeds of progress that brings about change. That one change always brings about another change. When winter comes, you don't still wear your summer clothes. You change your clothing according to the seasons. Summer clothes for summer, and winter clothes for winter. You dig? When you leave that person because they were dead weight to you, what usually happens? That person has a free range to live their life, and do whatever the hell they want to do. But No! Them negative motherfuckers wants to remain the same, and when you leave them for greater things you are the blame. They will try to fuck your world up! But negativity and bullshit will never stop a real stepper!

This is the reason why successful people and rich people become rich and successful, they know that dead weight will pull them down with it. So the successful people in this money game know that a consumer or customer mindset is not how you become successful in the money game. So if you or your partner are always finding shit to buy, and never seek to invest, then you are with a uncontrollable consumer, or with an emotional customer. That means you are in partnership with dead weight, your not a entrepreneur, nor a capitalist to continue to stay with a dead weight person that fight against you instead with you and for ya'll to win. That means the money bag will be heavy and stuffed with cold hard cash, A+ credit scores, and money will always be thrown to the successful and rich people from the banks. While you put your money in the banks for the serious capitalist and entrepreneurs to use for their goals, vision and a new lifestyle. Smart people play the money game, and cut those dead weight people loose that's holding them back and keeping them down. Successful people and rich people know they have to get rid of their dead weight fast, quick and in a hurry. Time is of the essence with people that play this money game. So the rich and successful are living the life you claim you want too, but they are doing it different and thinking different than you. Peep Game!

Control and Management

If you are unable to control what and how you think, then you will not be able to control your actions nor your behavior. If you can't control what you think and how you act, then how in the Hell are you going to control your bad spending habits and your bad money management? We will wait for you to answer that question. We been there! Yes, of course we fucked off plenty of money, and that's why we are more than qualified to inform you and warn you about the importance, of what and how you think effects your life and your kid's future. How? With those bad warped habits and bad money management! Most of you fail to understand that money attracts money, and the lack of money attracts other people that also lacks having money. If you had a $10,000 stack of money right now in your hands with a good money management mindset, that $10,000 will turn into other $10,000. See, we have come to the conclusion, that what you had once before you can have it again, if you learned your lesson. We learned our lesson, and we still are reading those necessary books and listening to the right people. If you didn't learn that money lesson, then you will keep repeating the same shit until you do or don't. No one can get their financial lessons, if they are not willing to do what it takes to understand their financial mistakes. To be successful you must do things different, in order for you stop repeating those costly money mistakes. A person with a willing mindset and a strong desire can change their thinking and their behavior over night. All successful people and rich people have righted their wrongs, because their desire was too strong to resist success and the reward that comes with success and riches. When you fail to control your thinking, you will not manage your money correctly in order for you to have more of it. Money demands intelligence on how to use it, and also a shrewd mindset for business to keep getting money.

Another thing is most of you are hooked on the paper money, instead of the actual money game. See today real money is not paper, it's digital. In other words, money is numbers. Peep this! If you have a damn good credit score, which are numbers these banks will throw money at your feet without you calling and begging them for money. With a good credit score, a positive mindset, and good money management you will never be without money. The money will remain with you at all times. And man that is a fucking damn good feeling! If you get your credit score up, then you can use that money to invest money, to have more money and be in the money game. That's how you keep more money in your possession to really and truly enjoy life. Paper money will only take you as far as your thinking capacity, and your understanding on how to use it. The value of your money is what you do with it. The way you think about money, and what you think money is will determine the way you use it. We see money as our employees, meaning we put our money to work, in order to have more employees for bigger productions and more companies to invest into and with. This is call partnership and part ownership.

When you are unable to control yourself, then you will never be be able to control anything, but you will be controlled by other things and some people. As the saying goes, *"the person that can master their thinking and themselves, will be able to control others."* Many of you were told and taught that the rich and wealthy people are evil, and also that the *"love of money is the root of all evil."* Now here's what a Master Mind said in the Bible of Luke 16:9 NIV, *"I tell you, use worldly wealth to gain friends for yourselves, so that when it is all gone (the money) you will be welcomed into their eternal dwellings."* When you can't control your thinking, then you will not be able to control, nor manage you hard earn money. If you can't manage money, then you will not have money to invest, nor be among those that know how to use money and also know how to make money.

Many of you twisted suckers and lame-bastards try to control your women and chase pussy, before you know how to control yourself and your money first. If you control your thinking and your dick with good money management, you will have more women chasing you than a bitch *(female dog)* has flees. Or better yet, women and pussy will be all over your ass like funk on shit! When you can control your thinking and your dick, with good money management, you won't have to be a trick or a sucker for a woman. If most of you women would learn how to control your emotions with intelligence, then you will have the man you need and want. That same man will be able and willing to bring you that heart felt happiness you desire so greatly. Control and money management is one of the major keys to success and money in this money game. We don't mean to be too blunt or swear too much! We just aiming to bring and gave you dear reader, the Raw Truth, so you can see the Game from a far, and play the game well up close. Can you dig it?

Financing your Lifestyle

Alright lets get into it. Before with get down to business, we must understand what is finance. We will break it down for you like this, finance is the knowledge and the understanding of applying economical science of managing your money, within a system of operation for you to begin your wealth building. We talked about money management earlier, and why and how you should learn to manage your money so you can keep most of it. Once you are able to manage your money, next is the financing that comes with money management. The way you use your money, is also how you are financing your lifestyle. If your money is not being financed within or with some investing financial institution, or even put to work for an idea, product or service, then you will be financially struggling or broke.

Here's one example, say for instance you went to the dealership to buy a car, and the salesman set up a real good deal for you. Then, when you get to the financing department some things appear to be misunderstood concerning the numbers and what you told the salesmen. And the salesmen always says, *"I was giving you a ballpark figure, but I'm not the financing guy. He handles all that with the banks."* The finance guy tells you what the bank is going to finance the car you want for such and such many years, and this is the payment plan. They also explain how much you should put down for this monthly payment, or if you don't put any money down, then your monthly payment will be this. Next, he pulls out this long form that breaks down where your money went, where your money is going, and how your money is put into certain categories or systems to finance the car. This is a great strategy and tactic when it comes to using your money and financing your lifestyle. You see we go into these places of business, and sign papers and make deals. The most shocking thing is, we never really pay close attention to how they are doing things in order for the business to remain prosperous and productive for so many years. If we would just study those systems it will give us not only a blueprint on how to manage and finance our lives for success and possible riches. It will provide for us the ways and means to be setup for life. Do you know how long some of these car dealerships has been in business? And the most important thing is yourself, some of the people you know and ourselves included, we don't buy cars everyday or very often. We don't even want a car note! So how is it that these car dealerships are able to last this long? It's because they have a strong proving money system. That system is for the business to manage the money intelligently, work with other prosperous and sound money businesses, and the financing operation is also set up for the business to make more money. Sometimes these car dealership businesses will have to merge with another profitable dealership business. Only if that particular car dealership has to in order for it to survive, and the merger is worth the process. Meaning is it profitable!

There's a guy we both know some people call him FOE, we call him CEO. This guy is one of the sharpest and meanest barber we have ever seen that ever touched a pair of hair clippers. This guy has people coming from the north, the west, the east and part of the south, and the deep south side of the city of H-Town for him to cut their hair in any style and any fashion. But here's the point, this guy was so determine to be his own Boss, he did what all serious minded capitalist and focus entrepreneurs do. He saved most of his money, he also managed his money, and then he financed his own shop. Meaning he put his money into a system and operation for him to be a Boss among Bosses. That's what we call managing and financing your lifestyle. He has left his kids a blueprint for success, generational wealth and wisdom. That one business with his good money management, good people skills, talented barber, and money discipline granted him another door of opportunity. And that was for him to open up another business. We are showing you some sound tactics and strategies that it can happen for you, if you would do the necessary things to make it happen for you. No one is going to do it for you! Opportunities will fly at your feet, if you are serious about doing and being what you claim. Nature don't give a shit about your intentions, nature is always in motion. What does that mean? That means nature or better yet, Mother Nature acts all the damn time. Just like during the cold seasons people tend to speak nuisance, like for example. They would say something like this, *"The grass is dead."* The grass is not dead, the vibration in the earth, which is the soil mineral and elements are moving slow. Mother Nature is always speaking to those that understand what they see and hear without a word being spoken. If you think buying books, and going to college is too expensive and reading is worthless, *"keep being ignorant."* Think about all the money you have blown from not knowing how to make more money and how to keep more of your money. Reading those financial and money management books, you will cut out your stupid bad spending habits. By buying one book a month, you could learn how to use your money, that could possibly save you an extra $100 a month or $1,200 a year. The book can show you how to invest to turn that $100 a month into $200, and that $1,200 a year into $2,400 and on and on to the real money bag.

#31 STRATEGY

Money, Sex and Power

Money is powerful within itself, but it is too powerful in the wrong hands, because it will not be used right. Sex is also a powerful feeling. Sex is a very powerful feeling that can and has driven some people to committing acts of violence, deceit, lying, becoming a nympho-manic, rapist, domestic violence, teenage pregnancies, dead beat parents, sexual tricks(*customers that pay for sex*) and selfish marriages, due to the power of physical sex. When you know how to use money, you can become a powerful person. See, money has an energetic pull on the psychology of all people. What do we mean by that? Whether that person is financially broke or has millions of dollars, when that money reaches their hand or account, they will feel that surge of energy that money brings. Some people call it financial freedom, some call it financial security, but we call it our employees. Money is also a form of sex to the brain, because it gives the person that euphoria within their brain mechanics. It causes the brain to release dopamine, which is the chemical that is being released when the physical sexual act is being performed. This is why the wealthy white people and the rich black people are rich and successful, because they have gotten really high from their success. They are hooked and they are addicts about success, money and power. So, basically they have trained their brains to think successful, which is the next business tactic and strategy for their next high. Successful peoples' brains are so wired to doing what it takes, to get that successful high from thinking outside the box. They are very energetic with a positive mindset within the business world. Peep Game! That is why successful people and rich people thoughts are always moving like the speed of light, when it comes to seizing opportunities to making deals. Successful people and rich people don't worry about failures, loosing money, because the lesson and their actions is greater than a dollar. Dig this! Majority of the people that are not successful always hesitates when it comes to making money deals and seizing business opportunities. Successful people and rich people are always merging with bigger businesses and socializing with successful people and rich people. Poor people can only socialize with other poor people. Poor people lack the power of thought, but poor people love the power of physical sex. Successful people and rich people love the money game, and making more money for their lifestyle. That comes from them always having intercourse with other successful powerful people. Now, when we speak on intercourse we are not talking about physical sex. We are talking about the *"act of entering a course of action and thought."* Because we as humans always have to enter into something with action for a reason and purpose for entering the course, performing the act or the place. Check this out, when you start saving money, and you start with $5. Over time when the money that you are saving begins to grow, it does something great to the brain. Not only does it bring you financial happiness and inner gratification, it stimulates your brain wires. This stimulation is the first step to getting high on money. The more money you save the more you are getting high off money. This is how you program yourself to always having and getting more money, because it stays in and on your mind. The power of money and the sexual intercourse with money, leads to the power of always wanting and desiring more money euphoria. Getting money is a great sexual act between positive and negative thinking! Getting money is also a great sexual act between taking action or staying complacent. Success is a sexual act between learning the game of money or staying ignorant of your potential not to grow. Getting money is a great sexual act between investing and spending it on bullshit! You get the idea? If you can wire your brain to think about getting money the way you feel about sex, you will have money, sex and power. Then you will enter this world of success and riches. Majority of people today that are not successful, nor rich enjoy the power of having physical sex too much, which wears down their bodies and mental brain power. Without them realizing it they are training and programming themselves to be lazy, tired all the time and lacking the power to execute. In other words, they will spend most of their time laying up, thinking that's some big stuff just to bust a nut. Then when a baby or child comes up, due to an unwarranted or an unplanned pregnancy, the male, not the man runs from his responsibility, but wanted all of the sexual feelings and gratification. It becomes a whole lot of drama, because of some loser made a woman a mama, when he wasn't man enough to be a father from the start. Unsuccessful people fail to understand how powerful people and rich people stay in powerful positions and obtain their riches. Their lifestyle of playing the money game is how they get money, have sex and obtain power. You must take the time and make up your mind, in order for you to receive those powerful rewards for making smart investments that can lead to generational wealth. But you must start today, not tomorrow! Successful people and rich people know tomorrow isn't promised to them. But the lame brains always assume that tomorrow will be there for them. And that's why they waste too much time, because they believe they will always have tomorrow to do what they can do today. The money game requires you or anyone that desires to enter this world the power of thought. You must be money smart, a dedicated hustler, put in time for reading books on money, and most of all program your brain to start obtaining financial information continuously. You must learn and train your brain to making money deals, and you can do that on your smart phone. Begin talking shop with people that are more successful than yourself. Rich people and successful people are successful and rich junkies when it comes to their lifestyle and playing the money game. Can you dig it?

When it comes to porno flicks that shit is so addictive and most people don't know why. The person that continues to watch that X-Rated shit are getting a sexual high within their own brains. Whatever you train or program your brain to think with a powerful feeling, your circuitry or energetic currents in the brain are getting powered up and high-powered from that sexual stimulation over and over again. The brain will automatically become programmed to wanting, and needing that chemical release from what you are engaging your brain into. Right now while you are reading this book, you are getting high on this successful power and strategic stimulation. We want you to be a successful addict, that way you are always programmed to doing, and always being successful without you thinking very deeply about doing anything. Now you are programmed to perform for success on auto-pilot! You see how and why we are programmed to always be thinking ahead, because we are successful junkies. We love this shit! Not just for ourselves, but we damn sure understood that it was going take us to make those changes for our families, and the next generation and the generation after that. See the more we hustled and got money, our minds were plugging into the power source with the idea of success and money. The higher we were getting off success and money, the more we wanted more of it, because we were addicts and addicted to success and money about having those successful sexual acts *(successful actions)* and more money. Boy that mental sexual act of getting that money bag is powerful! That's why we love having sucessful intercourse with success, successful people, with investing money and getting more money, by being and staying powerfully programmed for more success and definitely more money.

We will end this chapter with a story, when a cheese junkie was blowing his horn he said, *"Man this cheese is better than sex!"* I thought he was a damn fool, but when research was done he was right on point. He made me a better womanizer, a Stoic, a street philosopher, a serious orator, and a damn good sophist, and the title was given to me, P. Lōs "The Wiz." Dig this! If you would just change your thinking about money, in other words have an intercourse with money, and if you want power, you must control your physical action of sexual intercourse. You must control how you use your money, and last but not least, you must train and program yourself to having positive powerful thoughts. The money game will always be played by those they are in the game for the financial benefits of money, sex and power!

#32
STRATEGY

Your Truth is the Freedom to Success

The truth we are talking about and mentioning here, is the truth we had to come face to face with also. If we didn't face our truth that set us free, we would not have written this book and made our money work for us. If we didn't face our truth we could have never got on this road of success. We would have never invested our money to be in a better position, if we didn't face our Truth that set us free to achieve our success. When you are in bondage psychologically, emotionally, and spiritually, then you will also be in bondage economically. Your bondage is your prison or jail without actually having real bars. Those bars are your mind and your emotional blockage to see and recognize your freedom and success. Bondage is the human lock-down that hinders, and stops any person from enjoying a good financial life. Bondage also will block you from having a life of happiness with success. Bondage hinders numerous of people from investing and playing a part in this money-market to make money. Since we confronted our truth years ago, which was to acknowledge our bondage we were able to set ourselves free from what was holding us back from moving forward. And boy, it is peaceful, productive and good to our minds. We can create, build, live and invest with a sound mind. That's what every real man needs in order to be a builder. That's why we wrote this book for those that are seeking help, and have a strong desire to be better in their lives. When you are free from your bondage you can do big things with your life. So we are an example of what can be done, and what will happen when you confront yourself with the Truth. When you come face to face and acknowledge that truth that you have been denying for so long, you must act on that Truth that stares back at you in the mirror every morning. When you are really sick and tired of that same cycle of not progressing, and dealing with the same stupid shit from someone in your life, you must do something about it. The truth that you confront becomes your strategy and tactic on how to make your Exodus. Be truthful with yourself for yourself, that there is a bondage in your life and it is effecting your life negatively.

In order for you or anyone to be free from their financial setbacks, emotional hangups and being on that money struggling cycle, which is that hamster's wheel of going nowhere, you must confront your truth and do something about it. If you refuse to do something better for you, then do not look for someone else to do better with you. What you refuse to do for yourself, is the door you will open to someone to do what they please and want do for themselves. They will capitalize off your vulnerability, your lack of self-esteem, your lack of confidence in yourself and your self-denial for greatness. Can you dig that? When you don't know your great capabilities you are denying your God-given power to be great. Dig this, *"greatness denied, is a life with talents that hasn't been applied."*

There are males that let their women run all over them, and when they come around other men talking that big-ego talk about leaving her or putting her in her place. The more he talks about leaving her the longer he will stay with her. Because talk doesn't do much compared to action. We all have said, *"that action speaks louder than words."* Then why will anyone sit down and try to reason with someone that shows you daily there is no reasoning with them point blank? The truth of the matter is this person fails to confront the truth and acknowledge their truth, when they feel and see their reality slapping them in the face. You know what you need to do, which is leave her ass! But what do most of those weak men and weak people do in this type of situation? They stay there and put up with those bitch problems, or stupid emotional mommy's-boy male problems and hope for a better difference. Their difference is their solution, which is to make their personal Exodus/exit from him or her that has their ass in bondage. That bondage is staring them right in the face, and shaping their lives to be nothing and nobody! The truth will always penetrate the mind and heart. Here it comes! The man that fails or denies to leave his female bondage, will be the man that will never live with freedom and have a peaceful mind to build, create and be wise. Dig this! The man that never grows wise, knowledgeable with understanding, will never be a God in his woman's eyes, nor his children's lives. That is what we call and also know as deep respect. When your kids and your woman know that they can count on you, that is when you are in your God Space and living in your Royal Place. The person that truly believes in God, know they can count on God, that's why they believe in a God. Can you dig that? So what's the strategy? We will give you a little more.

Make plans and see them plans inside and outside. You must anticipate and assume a greater outcome for yourself. You must believe deep down that you are making One of the Greatest moves you have ever made in your life. Because freedom can never be bought, sold and definitely not abused. From that point see yourself on your mountain top! Stack as much bread as you can before you make your Exodus. Ask a family member or a close friend can you bunk with them, and you will help them with the bills until you get on your feet. If push comes to a fucking shove, get yourself a motel or an efficiency economy apartment. We are showing you there are many ways to leave the bullshit for greatness. I myself went through this, and I didn't let nothing stop me. Because I knew deep down, that I was going to be a better man for myself, my kids, my woman, my business partners, and also remove that emotional strain from my mother's emotional psyche. I Am on my Square, I meet other successful brothers and sisters on the Level. I Am working with my Plumb, and I always part on the Square. In other words, I play the Game fair. One last jewel for you! When you leave, you better make damn sure that you are sure and will never accept abuse and bullshit again! If you don't stand on it and you crack, that sucker will be back in your life doing the same dumb bullshit by your permission. Only because you have shown the person that you don't mean what you said and what you did. They are under the impression that you are still weak for them, and you ain't shit without them. Either face your Truth or die in bondage. We don't mean physical death! We mean a deep psychological and emotional death, which is suffering while you live. The Truth that you will no longer deny, is the same Truth that will set you free from your bondage.

The Upper Room of All Strategies

In the introduction we told you that we were going to consume your mind with Wisdom, Knowledge and Understanding. We will admit that this last strategy, will go over numerous of peoples' heads. It will challenge many readers to think different and consider somethings, but it will give Light beyond Light to the serious seeker that's willing and ready to use their Godhead on this playing field call planet earth. God is always Good when you use God's creative Wisdom, Knowledge and Understanding, where all Strategies are concealed from the Lames, Blamers, Abusers, Confusers, Excusers and the Losers. If you read the 32 strategies with an open mind, then you are ready to get down to business and play this money game like a Master. All real Masters, "*work from the sweat of their brows.*" Can you dig it?

In the Bible of Genesis, which only means the beginning of your Inner Genius. Have a little patience and mainly be patient with yourself for yourself. We are giving you the Key to open that Great Door to achieve your Greatest Good. In the Book of Genesis 1:6, NKJV Then God said, *"Let there be a firmament in the midst of the waters, and let it divide the waters from the waters."* What is this firmament that is in the midst of this water, and where is this water? This firmament is when the Light within your mind comes on with a strong conviction, when you are thinking on a Higher level and creating with this firmament. Look closely at the word *firmament,* and you get *firm;* meaning to be stable, steadfast, and solidly determined. Next, you get the letter *a* and last *ment*, which is mentality or *mental* =mind. We hope we didn't loose you! You may ask what does all of that have to do with the money game? If your mind isn't firm enough, dedicated and committed to your intellectual creative ideas on how to get money strategically, then you will never get enough money to live a better constructive life. The first waters that is mentioned is the water where your brain sits within your skull. This water is your chemical electromagnetic waters/ electrical currents/ which is the waters that surrounds the brain. This water is those chemical fluid neurons(*nerve cells*) in your brain. When these nerve cells are triggered with a creative idea, the waters are rippled with currents from that thought or idea, and the mind will get fired up and inspired, that becomes your firmament in your Upper Room. This Upper Room is your Head/Mind that is separated from the waters in your body. This is what you have to Understand in order for you to play the game of money. Every paper bill and every coin has a Head on it. Do you think that is a coincident? We made mention of that also. The Head is the most important thing that must be organized. If your thinking and your thought process isn't organized nothing else in your life will be organized.

Also in the Book of John 1: 1-5, NIV *"In the beginning was the Word, and the Word was with God, and the word was God,"* When we speak we use words, and those words come from our brains, our thoughts, our thinking, and from some people Intelligent Higher Minds. The words that come from our brain, is also the words that come from the God of your thinking, thoughts, brains and your mind. God is the Masculine Highest Principle of Thought and Thinking! The words you speak, and the thoughts you think, is how you create your world, because you are using certain words when you speak, only because you are thinking in a certain fashion. This fashion acts in accordance with your Inner mindset that formulates your conception and shapes your daily outer perception of the life around you.

How you mentally conceive things is how you deal with them, so you can be able to handle the things the way you perceive the things to be. In the beginning was the *word*, which is the thought, thinking and this is how you put things into motion; creating. And the thought or word was with the God of your imagination. Meaning whatever and however you believe your God to be, is how you use your God of thinking from within. And your God will use the materials, the people, the money and other needed materials to form, shape and create the world outside from the world it sees from within. You create yourself*(man/woman)* from of your likeness on how and what you think yourself to become, by how you using your Godhead. No matter what you believe, or what you were taught to believe you are still creating your world from within you first, and then the world around you second, by the way you think about yourself for yourself. The word imagination is also where we get the word image. Dig this! Within the word *imagination* you see the word *image*. The word image literally means a picture, a form, and a shape, that can only be described by the words you think and speak, that comes from within the mind of your thought-form. So, if you can't imagine yourself being successful and shape that world of success within you, then you will never live or be what you can't see for yourself from within yourself for yourself. Can you dig it?

So the way you see God from within you, is also how you shape the man/woman(yourself) from within you and the world around you. Your world is your very mind, not this whole damn planet! This is the Greatest Strategy that all serious players have used to achieve their success according to their image, and by the way they think and utilize their brain electrical frequency. In other words, their Godhead! Now, when we go a little further in this same Book of John. 2) *"He was in the beginning with God."* I know many of you were told, taught and indoctrinated to believe that this *He* was and is Jesus. You are wrong and totally erroneously Wrong! The word *He* is emphasizing the masculine dominating principle of creative thought. That idea within you has to dominate your very Mental Being, in order for you to firmly execute from the idea that is consuming your very thoughts and feelings for action. The Firmament of a Potent and Powerful mindset is what you need for you to enter this money game and play it strategically well! The *Mind*, *Golgotha*, and the *Nous* is Unlimited with great possibilities of ideas, tactics, ideals and strategies to create and achieve. Remember the *Word* is what gives life to the brain or mind of ideas. The powerful mind of Words*(images)* was with God and is God, which is your thinking in the beginning of your thought before you spoke and acted. 3) *All things were made through Him, and without Him nothing was made that was made."* Every thought that you think with a strong conviction and you acted on it, you have made your life to be what it is by Him(*dominate masculine thoughts*) that were strong conviction of thought and action. Everything that you did and you see around you wasn't a physical thing, until you thought it, acted on, and now it is made. Without a brain to think you couldn't carry out not one single act or movement to be in accordance with your line of thinking and reasoning to do what you did, in order for you to see what you have done. Conception *(thinking/thoughts,)* and Perception*(seeing/visual)*! Stay with us now! 4) *In Him was life, and the life was the light of men.* Remember the firmament is that Light, your thought, your thinking, your Mind, which is that light of consciousness that gives everyone that Light of Life for a Higher and Greater life. 5) *And the light shines in the darkness, and the darkness did not comprehend.* When that light(firmament) of ideas comes on within you to do what you see to do, is why it is the Light. Because what you didn't know or see before, now when that Inner Awareness that came on, now you are able to see and comprehend what you didn't understand nor comprehended once before. That's why when some people that have tried to understand something that was new or complicated from the start, and they didn't truly comprehend the thing or they misunderstood the thing, and then later when they get it, they exclaim with great joy, *"I See now!"* Can you dig it?

Darkness is ignorance or mental blindness! This is the reason *they can easily pull a wool over your mind and eyes, by "social engineering"* your thoughts and feelings, in order for them to shape your world for them and by them to win. Your enemies know how to play this game, and that's why they are winning in this money game. When a person ignores their truth, they are literally and mentally blind and unable to see, due to their Light of creative thought for a better life is out. That person will move, act, speak and have their being in their ignorance, which is in their darkness of restricted and limited thoughts of thinking, being and becoming. The person that speak on limitations, is the same person that will live and remain small within their circle of life with limitations. You and no one can play this money game strategically, while being and operating (thinking) in the darkness of their thoughts and their thinking. These are the people that the jail cells were built for, and a life continuous struggle and unhappiness will consume their very existence. That's why there are many youngsters and so-call adults that are moving and do things in the shadows(night time) of their life. They are trying to hide from their preconceived plotting, planing and scheming to commit small stupid crimes, but you can't hide from you. Especially, when you know what you are doing is wrong from the start. That's why you are doing it in the dark, because your thinking is in the darkness, so you act in the dark. Negligence, UN-Creative, Unconscious to the greater and better things in life. The most strategic person can commit and do the most damage right before eyes, only because they know what you don't know. What you don't know, is what you can't conceive to know in order for you to perceive what is to be known.

This last strategy is why it's very important for you to start with the first strategy; *"Getting down to business concerning you"* first and foremost. You can never change someone else, before you have made those necessary changes within you first. In the Book of Mathew 7:3, NKJV *"And why do you look at the speck in your brother's eye, but you do not consider the plank in our own eye?"* This is one of the major issue that is holding some of us back, and causing some us to push others away that can be helpful in fulfilling our life time dreams, economical visions and those short and long-term goals. Small minded people don't have goals, a purpose and visions, and they are usually the ones that is always blaming others for their loss, and they are the ones that are lacking when it comes to doing something they need to do. We did this in order for us to be in this money game. We got down to business with ourselves, so we can be in business among businesses as players in this money game.

If you don't do anything concerning the first strategy, the the second strategy of, *"Picking your battles and Winning your War",* will cause your life to be a living Hell. You will never have peace of mind, because you fail to understand and know the difference between your battles and your wars. This will lead you to have all types of internal and external battles and wars that will be going on in your life, and negatively effecting your life and stopping you from having a better and brighter life. This chaos will trickle down to your kids, and they will believe this is what life is all about. I been their when I was dealing with a few females back in the gap. They thought and truly believed, that since I didn't slap them around or put my foot in their asses, something was wrong with me. In reality it was something wrong with them, and they admitted that's what they saw their parents do and how their parents related to one another. Fuck that! I am not going to jail for no domestic violence, because of someone's warped thinking and fucked up feeling is their definition of love by being physically abuse, verbally abused and mentally abused. That's stupidity! This type of living is what these kids are imitating, acting on and emulating, because that's all they see and that's what they grow up to believe within their undeveloped minds. This usually leads to an early tragedy in their young lives. Only because their so-call adult parents fail to understand and know the difference from their battles, and their goal setting War. Must parents fail to confront their Inner demons of thoughts and emotional pain of hurt that needs to be truly understood, so they can do something grand for themselves. This grand successful thinking and acting will shape their child's mental world to be better coming from a sound and solid good start. The right attitude and the right mindset is what is needed in order to be, act and achieve the outcome that is consuming the person to be a King or Queen on this chessboard game of life for the money bag.

When you think and move like a King or Queen, you will be able to utilize strategy number four. Only the person that thinks on the grand scale of things can be able to see those most needed details, that entails what, whom, where, and when to carry out the strategy that needs to be tactically done precisely without sloppiness, and most of all undetected. This is how all real Chess Masters play the game! They move Masterfully and cleverly with keen understanding by looking into the details of their opponents. This is how the Masters are able to outwit and outmaneuver their opponents mentality, by understanding the moves from their opponents moves that entails how and what they are thinking.

When you are able to see and truly know the details and what the entails are, then you will see how you can open the door of opportunity to fly with the Eagles that are successful and leave the buzzards, and those that choose to be unsuccessful behind. You can't join the winners thinking and believing and acting like a timid sheep, and waiting for an opportunity like a buzzard waiting for their meal. The Eagles are powerful enough to make and create their world to be what they need for them to have what they want. By their keen sight they can spot a mouse in a tall grassy meadow or pasture, and spot their meal from 10,000 to at least 20,000 feet above sea level, and swoop down and grab their meal with the greatest of ease. When you use what nature has given you to use, you provide and protect yourself, by utilizing what nature has giving you to become successful. The wolves utilize their power by grouping and gathering and being undetected until their prey is totally vulnerable. Real players know they have to act sly at one time or another to get in this money game. We didn't say break laws, we said be sly! Know how to get in the game, when you see and know for a surety that you are being slowly pushed out or initially kept out by the haters, the liars and them time wasting doubters. We are not going back through all of the strategies, just those ones that are most needed for the outset, or in the beginning. Strategy number six is very important, because this consist of you spending your life with a person that can possibly waste your time. "Picking the right Mate, is a possible Check-Mate," in this money game.

We have been planning and been economically strategic for years and years with our money. Like we said before, when you get yourself together first, and then your God-given power will bring an opportunity that will always come from somewhere and someone. That's why we were truly blessed to have a very successful partner from Selma, Alabama. Our brother and business partner Sumo. This brother was a blessing in disguise, until we sat down and chopped up. From those sit downs many ideals and ideas for us to be participants in the money game for that money bag is totally paying off. This brother has utilized these strategies in the past and he using these strategies now. By applying these strategies with his great understanding, and also utilizing his Inner Firmament, or the Great Light of thinking within his Godhead, it has as made him a serious business minded person. He was able to get himself together, and be on his Square, and shine that Great Light on his life partner(wife). She saw the Wisdom more than she heard it, and she picked up the Light, and became and is his much needed reflection of success by she being his Queen/ Moon. They have become two of the greatest organizers and Team in the city of Selma and in the state Alabama among their peers and in the business world. The same thing happened, when the brother Dj R/T Hemi and his mate opened up another business, which is a clothing boutique for women. When you get yourself together the right mate will come or the one that has been there will get themselves together to be successful with their mate. The conjoined power is a major move for them to be on the road to achieving generational wealth and success. That's by having the right Team-Mate and the right personal mate whether husband, wife, boyfriend or girlfriend is very important to being and becoming successful. Like the old saying in the business world, and it is very True, *"If you are hanging with 4 broke people you will most definitely be the 5th broke person."*

We truly and sincerely hope this book has been a great help to you, and also for you to achieve what you seek to achieve. These strategies were imperative and they still are very helpful for us to have been able to achieve our level of success. We are mature people with mature minds, doing our thing in order for us to leave something behind that is worth leaving for the next generation. It's time out for all that ignorant bullshit drama, that has been and still is a generational curse for black people all the around the globe. These generational curses is why many of us are struggling for money. This mental money struggle has caused many of us not to play the game fair. This cycle of unfairness keeps the brutes out of the real money game, so they become the players in their game of violence and ignorance. Then this becomes the normal destruction and death cycle. That leads to the Traps, Tramps and the Champs to leave that circle of nothingness. Nothing from nothing equals not a damn thing coming! Within our ghettos, torn black community and upside down black neighborhoods is everyday degradation, everyday gun shots that leads to a violent trip for hospitalization, black on black genocidal and daily homicide. This shit is forcing the big money players to buy up all the property in these run-down, backward torn-up black communities and unproductive Latino communities also. We truly don't get it, and that's why we never will have something worthy to pass down to our children's kids. They are renovating and rebuilding the dilapidated homes, apartment building and the convenient stores. This is the money game! Then after they clean up, kick you out, and created nice looking communities, they raised the rental properties monthly rents and the mortgages are so high you can't continue to live there anymore. You are forced out, only because you believed yourself to be small and insignificant, to participate in the money game. These serious money game players has been playing off your ignorance, and they are playing to win on and off your kids undeveloped minds. By you not participating in this money game there is no excuse! While you are believing that you are out of this game, you are deluding yourself! You fail to understand that you are being used by the players that has setup the game. They game was created by them, their rues are for them, and they are playing to win by their game and from them rules, and you are the pieces to be used. We hope you leave this Upper Room different and better, than when you first entered it. If you leave without feeling, and believing that you haven't changed a little, then study these strategies about yourself and for yourself again.

Conclusion

This money game has no conclusion, long as there are human-beings living, but we have to concluded with this book. There are many ways you can become a player in this money game by starting off small. When you begin small you will be able to remove your fears, start saving a little and begin investing a little, and learning the game over a period of time, in order to get your mind set on success. We invest strictly with the companies, that are innovative and growing with the times. This strategy was more strategic for us because we don't care what the market do or does, dig that! Because we are betting and investing with the company that has smart and ambitious players on the Team. The company utilizes our invested money for those much needed advertising campaigns and innovative ways to make more money. When we invested our money with those companies, we gave the company access to use our invested money. So when the company make those big profits we get a piece of the pie. The piece of the money and profit of the pie is call and known in the business world as dividends. Now these dividends is the money or the divided ends(money/dividends) is what we receive. When the company pays us some money back in dividends, we don't want our money back. You probably saying what! We reinvest the money(dividends) to let the company use more of our money, so we can make and have more money also. We automatically investing our money without thinking about it so we can purchase more shares of the company, and be in a more powerful position to play in this money game. This is also the reason why we invest to have a portfolio with a diversified money cushion with various companies nation wide.

Another thing you can do is setup a saving account to just save money, you will also need an emergency money account. You will need another money account to prevent you from pinching or touching that emergency account money. That's why you have to have numerous of money spots to prevent you from touching one of those money spots that will lead you back down the road you just got off of. Which is the road or street call the broke and money struggle dead end street. We know some of you are thinking this is hard. Yes it is hard when you don't have the right mindset for it. When you set your mind in order, then your mind will bet set on success and success will be yours. Because you are mind is set on that mental dial of success, and from then on your mind can only see, picture, imagine, conceive, think and be strategical for nothing but success.

We will leave you with this, in the Book of Romans 12:2, NKJV *"And do not be conformed to this world, but be transformed by the renewing of your mind, that you may prove what is that good and acceptable and perfect will of God..."* This is how Social Media and Social Engineering is keeping you broke. They got you thinking that buying all that big jewelry, the big luxury homes, expensive cars, expensive smokes(cigars), high priced liquors, high price purses and name brand bullshit is what success looks like. When was the last time or the first time you saw the 1% with this bullshit! What about the motherfuckers that's running everything you need and use for you and your family to survive and live? Those big money players in this money game know how to use material shit for more success, for more riches, for generational wealth and for more power? The Big Players know how to be strategical off you, from you and by you, only because they know what you know not! Many of you don't have a fucking clue, no matter how much you tell yourself that you do know what's happening out here. If you did you would only enlighten a few, and tell the rest on what they shouldn't know, so they can believe what they don't know! Dig that shit if you can! When you don't renew your mind, which is to think different and in order to be better, you will do and be the same. That boils down to getting what have gotten, and have what you always had. Nothing more, but surely a lot less than what you can be getting and having! You have to think different, to do different in order to be different from the pack, then you will become successful and possibly rich. If you continue to be around average motherfuckers majority of the time, you will be an average sucker. If you continue to be around broke motherfuckers you will be the next broke sucker. Listen Fam, we hope very sincerely that you truly understood, and dig that Psychological Skullduggery is the greatest strategy among the human world. We are extending our hands to pull you up with us and even Higher. We are Players in this Money Game for that Money Bag. You can continue to play Roulette on yourself and gamble your life away, the choice is your. We are definitely betting on Ourselves, like we always have and always will! Peace Fam; Success is Yours!!!

You need at least 3 types of incomes or money making strategies.

1) Earned income	2)Passive income	3) Portfolio income
Work on job	Real Estate	Stocks/ Bonds
self-employed	Writing Books	Paper Assets
	Writing music and movies	

4) Investor

Invest into companies

Buy companies

Capital Investments

If you wish to get at any of one us you can DM us:
IG / Instagram @ DJ RT HEMI
IG/Instagram @ plos1886

The lady's Bodied Boutique online clothing store:
www.Itbodiedboutiques.com

To order other books by the authors:
www.amazon.com/author/p.los
https://www.amazon.com> Swagggin-Hip-Hop-DJ-RT
OR
www.authorhouse.com

Recommended Reading

Are You Loving What Is Not Loving You?
By Delady

Swagggin' HIP-HOP
By DJ RT Hemi

The Game Remains But the Players Change
By P. Lōs

From the Streets to the Millionaire $eats
By P. Lōs

The Bible of The Game
By P. Lōs

Psychological Skullduggery
By P. Lōs

Printed in the United States
by Baker & Taylor Publisher Services